LYOTARD AND THE POLITICAL

Lyotard's work is somehow obviously political, but how? *Lyotard and the Political* demonstrates that it's not so obvious after all. James Williams does important and original work in helping us understand what determines the political for Lyotard – not the hype about postmodernity, and not just the experience of the differend and the obligation to bear witness, but the complicated and under-appreciated notion of libidinal economy. Returning to Lyotard's early work, Williams reconsiders libidinal economics to arrive at a reading of the political as 'active passivity'. His evaluation is at once passionate, severe, and provocative.

Thomas Keenan, Bard College

Lyotard and the Political offers the first systematic analysis of the political implications of the work of the highly influential and controversial French philosopher Jean-François Lyotard. James Williams clearly traces the development of Lyotard's thought from his early Marxist essays on the Algerian struggle for independence to his break with the thought of Marx and Freud. This is compared with Lyotard's later writings on the politics of desire and his highly influential attempts to base a postmodern political discourse on the sublime.

The book situates Lyotard's thought in terms of the dominant political and philosophical positions of the twentieth century, exploring the reasons why Lyotard lost his belief in revolutionary politics and the consequences, both negative and positive, of this loss. Williams particularly emphasizes Lyotard's relationship with Kant, Heidegger and Deleuze and illuminates the political dimension of Lyotard's writings on art, literature and style in philosophy.

James Williams is Lecturer in Philosophy at the University of Dundee. He is the author of *Lyotard: Towards a Postmodern Philosophy*.

THINKING THE POLITICAL

General editors:
Keith Ansell-Pearson
University of Warwick

Simon Critchley
University of Essex

Recent decades have seen the emergence of a distinct and challenging body of work by a number of continental thinkers that has fundamentally altered the way in which philosophical questions are conceived and discussed. This work poses a major challenge to anyone wishing to define the essentially contestable concept of 'the political' and to think anew the political import and application of philosophy. How does recent thinking on time, history, language, humanity, alterity, desire, sexuality, gender and culture open up the possibility of thinking the political anew? What are the implications of such thinking for our understanding of and relation to the leading ideologies of the modern world, such as liberalism, socialism and Marxism? What are the political responsibilities of philosophy in the face of the new world (dis)order?

This new series is designed to present the work of the major continental thinkers of our time, and the political debates their work has generated, to a wider audience in philosophy and in political, social and cultural theory. The aim is neither to dissolve the specificity of the 'philosophical' into the 'political', nor evade the challenge that 'the political' poses the 'philosophical'; rather, each volume in the series will try to show that it is only in the relation between the two that the new possibilities of thought and politics can be activated.

Volumes already published in the series are:

FOUCAULT & THE POLITICAL
Jon Simons

DERRIDA & THE POLITICAL
Richard Beardsworth

NIETZSCHE & THE POLITICAL
Daniel W. Conway

HEIDEGGER & THE POLITICAL
Miguel de Beistegui

LACAN & THE POLITICAL
Yannis Stavrakakis

LYOTARD AND THE POLITICAL

James Williams

London and New York

First published 2000
by Routledge
11 New Fetter Lane, London EC4P 4EE

Simultaneously published in the USA and Canada
by Routledge
29 West 35th Street, New York, NY 10001

Routledge is an imprint of the Taylor & Francis Group

© 2000 James Williams

Typeset in Times by Keyword Publishing Services Ltd
Printed in England by Clays Ltd, St Ives plc

British Library Cataloguing in Publication Data
A catalogue record for this book is available from the British Library

Library of Congress Cataloging in Publication Data

Williams, James, 1965–
Lyotard and the political / James Williams.
p.   cm.
Includes bibliographical references and index.
1. Lyotard, Jean François—Contributions in political science.
I. Title.
JC261.L86.W55   1999
320'.092—dc21   99-32750
                                                         CIP

ISBN 0-415-18348-0 (hbk)
ISBN 0-415-18349-9 (pbk)

For Rebecca and Nathan

CONTENTS

CONTENTS

ABBREVIATIONS

References to Lyotard's texts will use the following abbreviations:

DF   *Discours, figure* (1971)
DMF *Dérive à partir de Marx et Freud* (1973)
DP   *Des Dispositifs pulsionnels* (1980a)
PMC *The Postmodern Condition* (1984c)
JG   *Just Gaming* (1985a)
TD   *The Differend: Phrases in Dispute* (1988a)
IN   *The Inhuman: Reflections on Time* (1991a)
LE   *Libidinal Economy* (1993a)
PW   *Political Writings* (1993c)
PF   *Postmodern Fables* (1997)
SM   *Signé Malraux* (1996)

1

INTRODUCTION.
LYOTARD ON MALRAUX:
NIHILISM, ART AND POLITICS

One of the last books to appear before Jean-François Lyotard's death (Paris, 20 April 1998) marks a baffling departure. *Signé Malraux* (1996) is a biography of the French twentieth-century writer, political activist and politician André Malraux. Why write a biography at the end of a career as a writer on philosophy, art and society? Why a biography within an *œuvre* that is resolutely post-structuralist in its opposition to the modern dominance of the self and the subject and to positivist conceptions of truth? There is no object or subject 'André Malraux'; only a patchwork of books, influences, languages, events, structures. Even if there were, to capture such a figure with its intentions, beliefs, feelings and desires would tell us little about the genesis of literature, the significance and truth of art, or the importance and function of politics.

Signé Malraux, however, is not a simple biography. Lyotard calls it a 'hypobiography' (SM: 355). It goes beneath the figure and invents an André Malraux, one that expresses deeper movements and influences than could be divined from the life proper. He also calls it a work of 'mythopoïesis', that is, the artistic distillation of a figure from a mixture of heterogeneous elements: Malraux's novels, life, politics, subconscious, his friends, enemies, loves. The book is not afraid to invent in order to make a success of that expression. In response to those who already see here all that is corrupt and decadent in poststructuralism and in Lyotard's philosophy, in particular, I would say that *Signé Malraux* is a work of the new-found maturity of this relativist and hypercritical tradition. It shows Lyotard able to create a consistent whole and to speak through it, without having to deconstruct or self-consciously to undermine his own arguments and conclusions, but also without having to resort to the suspect devices of objectivity and positivism. It is understood that this is Lyotard's *Malraux*, a productive falsehood that operates on and tells the truth about much more that its eponym: 'Another document to add to the file of this connivance. Would I confess that it is a counterfeit? But mythopoïesis, as we shall see, makes the so-called "life".

1

The authentic is what it signs, not what a third party verifies or confesses' (SM: 19).

It is in the spirit of that maturity that I ask 'Why Lyotard's *Malraux*?' The question is put not to his intentions, but is one that helps to draw together the different strands of Lyotard's philosophical politics: his early essays on revolutionary Algeria; his cruel and passionate – and best – political works on libidinal economy; his most famous idea 'the postmodern condition'; and his most influential concepts on the most just philosophical and political testimony, 'the differend' and 'the sublime'. Lyotard's *Malraux* is a life and a set of works struggling to survive and affirm itself through the political terrors of the twentieth century. This is why it is Lyotard's; they share the struggle and the tools that make it possible: art, writing and a political life led on the margins.

Signé Malraux follows the key political steps of a modern struggle that is mirrored and condensed in Lyotard's life and works. Lyotard was a Parisian bourgeois academic. He taught philosophy at the Sorbonne, Nanterre, the University of Paris VIII (Vincennes, Saint-Denis). Later in his life, the reputation earned by his books extended his influence and teaching throughout Europe (Collège International de Philosophie, Paris), the United States (University of California, Irvine and Emory University, Atlanta) and academia worldwide. But that academic work has a political backdrop and topic. An early socialism allied to the revolutionary movements of strangers that have been lived with and loved (Algeria for Lyotard, Indochina for Malraux) is followed by an inescapable alliance of evidence for the base, ineffectual and terroristic nature of totalitarian politics on the left and on the right: 'We became intelligent just in time to see communism decline into an orthodoxy. . . . Our generation lived in the slow undermining or the catastrophic breakup of both liberalism and positivism' (PW: 87).

Neither Lyotard, nor Malraux, gives up on political action, but it could never be the politics of parties and factions. Malraux embarks on a quixotic attempt to form an air squadron for the Spanish Republic against Franco's German and Italian planes. Lyotard invites the hatred of his former comrades and colleagues as he writes and lives a libidinal philosophy of passivity to desires, free of the overseers of order, organisation and judgement: 'Politics, too, is an institution. Fringe group politics is a miniaturized institution. There is no difference between the security stewards of the March 16 meeting and those of the "Communist" . . . . The same goes for political discourse: there, too, a phraseology is handed down to us and we reproduce it faithfully' (PW: 49). The political, then, is never this institutionalised politics. It is a drive to act, understood as a necessity for a life, itself interpreted as an unstable relation of feelings, desires and structures. Lyotard does not define the political through its institutions or goals but as an attempt to respond to feelings and desires without falling back onto well-defined hierarchies of good and evil, them and us, origins and ideals, rules and laws, truths and falsehoods, fallen states and utopia: 'A first victory would be to manage to speak of these affairs without "talking politics"' (49).

This idea of the political as opposed to politics is doubly difficult. It gives *Signé Malraux* a heavy and tragic tone. First, how can one give consistency to life as an unstable relation without resorting to external structures that negate it? ('Thus the symbolic Father continues, under various imaginary costumes, to govern our words and our acts; thus the question of power among our ranks is always stifled, always displaced into the question of the power facing us.') The answer for Lyotard and for Malraux lies in art, both as model and as way. They think through art, act through art and live thanks to art; it is the possibility of life and the political. Three confusions must be avoided here. It is not that life and politics are art, in the sense of works of art – life as a novel, politics as theatre or spectacle. It is not that all lives and politics are art. It is not that all art is politics. Each of these views replaces one overbearing structure with another artistic one. Art, then, gives sense and direction to a life, gives rise to a politics of artistic representation, becomes the privileged political realm.

Instead, the sense of 'possibility' in the expression 'art makes life and politics possible for Lyotard' is one of providing an issue to a political and existential impasse: 'We don't even have the hope any more that what we stand for is a situation that remains to be created' (PW: 89). Two traits therefore dominate Lyotard's sense of the political as needful of art. Politics is no longer something 'we' – Lyotard, Malraux and those who share their sense of the political – can live with. Life can only be led where political action is artistic in its sensibility. 'We' must feel that action is necessary despite the death of politics. Art must testify to the necessity of the death of structure and institutions and yet still give rise to desires and passions, thereby providing us with a model for the political. This artistic creation – or, better, the act that accompanies this art – is the political act *par excellence*. Above all, this does not mean that either the political or art is defined primarily in opposition to institutions. Neither is even to be thought of as an alternative to them. Both are what makes it possible for us to live with institutions.

As a thinker of libidinal economy, Lyotard defines this possibility as a conspiracy for the political within politics. The libidinal, our desires and feelings viewed as equal partners in the economies that account for them and allow us to harness them, is to be released in the economic, thought of as any system of flow and exchange rather than as the economic proper. This equality concerns questions of dependence – no system without libidinal desires and feelings; no feelings and desires without systems. But, on matters of explanation, an unfamiliar asymmetry holds: we cannot fully explain or control the libidinal from within a system, for instance, by following a theory on the role of the passions in political economy. Lyotard observes one such

3

play of organisation and emergence of the libidinal in Malraux's haphazard creation of collections of art-works and books on art. Malraux passively allows a sometimes tawdry (the lassitude of an alcoholic neurasthenia), sometimes elevated, feeling (a fraternal love exceeding the roots we are given) to become expressed in the logic of the collection or in the flow of the book. This passivity is necessary. The obsessive control of passions and desires would kill the work, or at least subject it to further unseen libidinal precipitations and, worse, utterly negative desires of control and elimination. Against this negativity, Lyotard deploys what I shall later call a strategy of active passivity to conspire with the unpredictability of the libidinal and against the self-destructive urge of the economic to have done with the unknown or the unreal: 'It is nonetheless a constant that [Malraux's] novels, essays, prefaces and, above all, his studies on art ascribe revolt or creation to a force in man that exceeds him . . . the moment of humanism is placed under the aegis of the Unreal' (SM: 336).

As a thinker of the differend, or of an absolute difference between two sides of a conflict, Lyotard thinks of the possibility of living with the dumb weight of politics as a minimal resistance to an alliance of an illusory dialogical entente and capitalism. In the later years of his work – roughly, from the late seventies – he studies the feeling of the sublime that stops this false bridging between absolute differences. So his aim is to testify to the differend, the two sides of which are caught in a conflict that admits of no just resolution, that is, just from both points of view. The political must bear witness to this impossibility of a justice that brings both sides together; it is a political struggle against the imposition of a common ground where none exists.

So the feeling of the sublime must be set against ideas of reason, such as humanity, in order to stop them grinding difference into a mere marketable and productive variety, or into the terror of an obvious consensus ('Of course there is a right way, of course there is a way for me to understand you'). According to Lyotard, the feeling of the sublime halts our drives to understand, to judge and to overcome. It does not so much cancel them as leave them in suspense by welding to them feelings that indicate that a difference is impassable. Thus Turner's paintings of the *The Old Devil's Bridge*, *Pass of St Gothard* capture the bridge as a fragile line thrown between great alps that threaten to stretch, twist and throw it into the abyss at the faintest change in tumultuous skies. There is a bridge, but not one that you feel is passable. It is a sign that there is hope in fording the waterfall that has cut an irreparable gulf into the mountain, allied to a sign that the hope is in vain. But, because Turner works through feelings and the senses, the contradiction stands as long as his paintings capture us. They do not fall prey to the precept of logic that we cannot be in a state of simultaneous hope and despair. Again, art shows Lyotard the way to resist politics by adopting feeling at the heart of political acts.

But why resist or conspire at all? The second reason for the difficulty of the idea of the political that comes out of his work lies in the question of why this idea is at all necessary. Why is there a move in Lyotard from particular disasters of politics to a conspiracy within or resistance to institutional politics? Would not the most appropriate response to these disasters be an attempt to learn from them within politics? We should avoid the disasters, ward them off, shore up what has proven resistant to them. Perhaps some postwar liberal consensus offers such a politics, or maybe it lies in the cosmopolitan structure of human rights, or in a new multi-faith religious order, or even in the imposition of a local conception of truth, justice and decency because it is better than all others? None of these is taken up by Lyotard and some of his importance as a political thinker is as one of the most thorough critics of all these options. To liberal orthodoxies he opposes the capacity of capitalism to metamorphose itself each time its terroristic side is chained by politics and law. More than that, however, he is sensitive to the blackmail of capitalism: control it, and it will destroy itself, only to rear up again somewhere else with your craven assistance. To the others he responds with a double reminder of failure: you are nothing without capitalism because your foundations are necessarily unjust with respect to what they leave out or dismiss as other or different.

Yet, to take him merely as critic and devil's advocate is to miss the positive way in which he develops the political in relation to politics. His philosophy is not consistent with a regulative function within politics (as the negative that contributes to reason even as it is dismissed) because the drive behind his idea of the political is not primarily one of opposition. If we understand Lyotard as driven by a contrary and cynical will to show all that is wrong in politics, we misunderstand the drive behind the political. It is not that modern, institutional politics is mistaken, or wrong, or guilty, or contradictory in some straightforward intellectual sense, as if we could coldly identify this or that fault and decide whether it required surgery, rectification or an entirely new body politic. It is that, for Lyotard – for some 'us' – politics cannot be lived. This explains why he returns to Malraux, born twenty-odd years before Lyotard's birth (Versailles, 10 August 1924), but formed by the same century and the same philosophical, artistic and political senses of possibility and impossibility: 'No matter what it says, a political formation nourishes itself with and propagates the same deception: to believe or make believe that there is a remedy for non-sens' (SM: 173).

The word captured but also transformed by Lyotard's account of the impossibilities that govern Malraux's life is nihilism. Politics cannot survive nihilism, but the political can. The medium through which this struggle takes place is life. Does this commit Lyotard, this book and the political to an essential definition of life and to a determination of the political with respect to it? Not at all. Nihilism and life in *Signé Malraux* are given a floating definition. They are a cloak thrown over an indeterminate struggle between antagonistic ideas, drives and desires. This is not to say that definite, philosophical, definitions of nihilism are ducked by Lyotard or in this book on him; these appear in later chapters. More generally, the love of truth is still one of the main impulses in his work and the best way to approach the contradictions that arise in the search for the political as a resistance to or conspiracy within politics. But truth can itself be nihilistic, so his work is a questioning on two inseparable fronts: the political and the philosophical.

However, the reduction of this philosophy to abstract definitions, truths and arguments is also to be avoided. The following passages on life and nihilism from *Signé Malraux* help us to understand why:

> [André suffered from] a reality malady, much more serious than realism: a nihilist terror. Not nihilist thought, but a heart consumed by nothingness.
>
> (27)

> Here [in inter-war Germany and German art], unlike in Paris, they do not forget nihilist distress and suffocation. It is taken on, it becomes work. André immediately recognises that black force of separation . . .
>
> (87)

> . . . nihilism has worsened. Vast vision of a West destined to deepen its lack. But the size of the painting fails to hide its true motif, once again, a fear of language.
>
> (99)

> No, real death is the repetition of the whole movement, reproduction, the great Recount that life seems to contradict, with all its intriguing stories. Whilst, in truth, their noise harbours and covers the cycle's silence.
>
> (105)

> The same repeats itself, and the revolt against the same repeats it. A dreadful contraction, a despair, make Spain an echo of his most intimate suffering.
>
> (208)

For Lyotard, Malraux's nihilism is a complex of affects (terror, distress, suffocation, fear, dread and despair), ideas (reality, nothingness, separation, lack, repetition, separation) and sites (the heart, works, language, history, narratives, the political and social world – Spain, Indochina, the West). The complex and even its major constituents cannot be structured and organised, or abstracted into a set of definitions and rules or laws without losing their explanatory capacity over a full range of effects. The strength and beauty of *Signé Malraux* lies partly in the way in which Malraux's 'nihilism', understood as this indivisible complex of affects, ideas and sites, comes out of and explains his relation to women, to literature, to language, to places, countries and conflicts.

For an explanation of Lyotard's attraction to Malraux, the most important of these mutual relationships is with politics and the political, understood again as an act that refuses to hope for or be guided by an institution. A passage from *Signé Malraux* stands out in its reliance on the explanatory power of nihilism. It could be autobiographical rather than biographical, if that term were not as suspect when applied to Lyotard as when applied to Malraux ('Ah! You make me fall into biographical imbecillity. At my age . . .', quoted in Lançon 1996: 2). The passage uncovers the dominant nihilism in Lyotard's philosophy and his attempt to live with it:

> For [Malraux and Bataille], the resolution to see into the depths, the conviction that the self and discourse forbid true communication, that this only comes from extreme experience, on the borders of spasm, agony, the sense of sacrifice with no way back, give to their respective understanding of nihilism an analogical consequence . . .: only the inhuman, abject and innocent, and not the superhuman, can accomplish the murder of God because it nourishes itself from the rotting corpse.
>
> (SM: 244)

Truth and the political only escape nihilism when they are no longer thought of within the categories of the self, the subject and well-defined discourses. What we commonly understand as communication, as the transfer of meaning between subjects and, reflexively, from the self onto the self, is only an access to a nihilist truth. A truth 'for us' – that unleashes terror and nothingness into the heart and into language.

Lyotard's work has been a predominantly political attempt to think and defend the extreme experience on the borders of discourses as resistant to nihilism. The following questions reflect an enquiry into this attempt as it is pursued through the six chapters to follow:

1   What was still nihilistic in Lyotard's politics around the Algerian war of independence? What was the legacy of his dawning awareness of this nihilism?
2   Is Lyotard's libidinal philosophy merely a nihilist reaction to the disasters condensed in the example of Algeria? Or does a new and consistent sense of the political emerge there?
3   If this new sense is to be called 'active passivity', to what extent are its roots negatively metaphysical? Can there be a positive characterisation

of active passivity? To what extent is active passivity a mere surrender to capitalism?

4   Is the turn to judgement in Lyotard's philosophy of the differend a valid reaction to the lack of judgement in the libidinal philosophy? Does Lyotard's work on the sublime provide the basis of a possible politics?

5   Can Lyotard's work after the philosophy of the differend be defended on the grounds that it can fulfil a regulative function within a democratic politics?

6   Does the nostalgia of Lyotard's later essays resolve the problem of what the political could be? Is 'active passivity' a withdrawal from politics and from truth-claims?

2

IMPASSE

THE ALGERIAN DIFFEREND

One of the best applications of Lyotard's philosophy of differends to a political context is by Mohammed Ramdani in his long introduction to Lyotard's *La Guerre des Algériens*. The book is a recent collection of Lyotard's essays on Algeria for *Socialisme ou barbarie* written between 1956 and 1963 (these are for the most part translated in *Political Writings*). Ramdani deploys Lyotard's philosophy of language and his insights into incommensurability skilfully to show that, even in his early work, Lyotard's political aim was to testify to irresolvable differences. In this case, this is the differend between colonial power and indigenous population.

Ramdani's argument covers three of the most important aspects of the theory of differend – its legal, linguistic and affective versions. The tort done to the Algerian people will never be able to express the wrong done to it through the French law courts. The linguistic heterogeneity stands between the phrase regimen of the colonial power, whether in the cognitive regimen (what has happened here is . . .) or the regimen of justification (it is right because . . .), and the aesthetic regimen that expresses great suffering and loss. These regimens are marshalled by the stakes of two incommensurable genres: (a) the colonial economic genre, the stake of which is to increase measurable monetary wealth (even if this is in very few foreign hands); and (b) the Algerian cultural and pathological genre, the stake of which is to express the elimination of a tradition and the suffering of those who live through it or who are forced to be separated from it.

The importance of this argument is historical, political and philosophical. Ramdani argues that Lyotard's isolation of the Algerian differend allows for a more accurate and truthful account of the events of the Algerian war of independence. It can be turned against colonialist revisionary accounts that either deny the validity of the war or deny its justification through an appeal to the economic failure of independent Algeria. The war draws its validity from the differend: it is a just expression of the impossibility of expressing a wrong in any other way than *spontaneous* uprising. Spontaneity

9

is important here – as it is in Lyotard's essays on Algeria – in distinguishing a struggle that turns the legal, linguistic, military and diplomatic methods of the colonial power back against it and a struggle that refuses to adopt these methods precisely because they are the source of a deeper wrong. Spontaneity, then, betokens a movement that cannot be recognised and understood from within the system it rises against. It is not a miraculous moment, but one that has to be understood as having a passionate coherence only in retrospect and independent of accounts in terms of political ideology.

The theory of the differend also allows for a political argument to emerge. Ramdani contrasts Lyotard's politics of testifying to the differend and a left-wing politics of using Algeria within the broader struggle for international socialist revolution. Sartre's 'Stalinism' is singled out for a particularly strong critical attack in this context. Lyotard develops and explains this criticism further in the 'Dérives' chapter of *Dérive à partir de Marx et Freud* (15–17). Philosophically, the differend allows for feelings, or more properly affects, since we are transformed and made by these 'feelings', to emerge as politically primordial. In this sense, the expression of the differend becomes the proper goal of philosophy, as opposed to the search for a resolution to the conflict. Whether this implies that philosophy and a philosophical politics should not concern itself with goals such as a free and just Algeria is a matter to be considered below.

The great value of Ramdani's work, then, lies in the way it answers two familiar criticisms of the later Lyotard. These criticisms can be thought of as variants of familiar critical attacks developed against postmodernism and poststructuralist philosophy. In undermining claims to truth and validity, these movements are said to inhibit the development of consistent and meaningful politics. If it is not possible to determine the truth of a given claim or the validity of a given argument, then it is not possible to develop a responsible or tenable politics. All arguments will ultimately founder on conflicting claims that can only be 'reconciled' by an appeal to force. Any position will, in the final reckoning, become aware of the contingency of its aims and methods and will hence subside into cynicism and then nihilism.

Nietzsche's argument from *The Will to Power* is turned on his modern followers, just as it hangs beneath will to power itself: 'He who sees the abyss, but with an eagle's eyes – he who *grasps* the abyss with an eagle's claws: *he* possesses courage' (Nietzsche: *Thus Spoke Zarathustra*, 298). The point of Nietzsche's argument is that it takes greater courage to work through the risk of nihilism than to deny it in the solace of logical abstraction, false objectivity, lack of sensitivity, or faith in ideals: 'I do not call cold-spirited, mulish, blind, or intoxicated men stout-hearted. He possesses heart who knows fear but *masters* fear; who sees the abyss but sees it with *pride*'.

The opposition to false solace is exactly Ramdani's point. Lyotard cannot be criticised for not putting forward a truth on the Algerian war of independence, since his truth is the differend. But it is a difficult truth, as much about impossibilities as about foundations for political resolutions. An irresolvable conflict gives rise to the war; it will not go away with independence; it will not go away with a diplomatic solution or with defeat; it will not even go away with revolution. Any position that denies the differend between colonialism, defined by its economic stakes, and the Algerian people, as defined by a culture, tells an untruth and prolongs an injustice.

A second criticism falls at this point. To deny resolutions is not to deny action. We must act for the differend, and this means against those who cannot see it or refuse to see it. In *Dérive à partir de Marx et Freud*, Lyotard explains this through a distinction drawn between resistance and the political belief in a new and pure beginning. In this later evaluation of the work of *Socialisme ou barbarie* he seeks to underline the disillusionment of the group with traditional left-wing party politics and with liberal democracy. Both positions offer the illusion of a just world while implicitly living with the hegemony and injustice of capitalism. Ramdani uses Algerian and French writers and historians to illustrate Lyotard's point and to give a critical counterpoint to those positions that use ideas and abstraction to deny the differend.

This is the strong aesthetic and literary quality of Lyotard's philosophy and politics. His sense of encouraging a drift away from fixed forms of power and bureaucracy in capitalism is essentially aesthetic. Any movement that can count as resistance depends upon an affect triggered unconsciously in art-works but also in spontaneous uprising and whose success is a matter of chance (DMF: 21–3). The irresolvable conflict can only be testified to in a medium capturing the feelings and affects that permit the differend to appear without cancelling it in one or other of the genres involved in the conflict:

> These texts [the novels of Kateb Yacine, Mouloud Mammeri, Jules Roy and Mouloud Feraoun and the histories of Mohammed Harbi and Albert Memmi] dramatise a tort, a differend between colonialist and indigen, that cannot be said in the language of the oppressor. But there is also a tort because the indigen has been judged according to norms and criteria, in a language and a culture, from a universe of thought that are not his.
>
> (Ramdani 1989: 14)

But an aesthetic medium is not the only one for the expression of the differend. Affects have to be communicated, but they must also be created anew. What this means is that although the suffering and loss of the Algerian people demands a mode of communication that does not hide it in the all-pervasive language of the colonialist, the differend as affect also

11

needs to be triggered in the outsider: it must be felt, in order to be recognised. This feeling is essential to Lyotard throughout his work: it identifies that something is happening that cannot find full expression in what is being said. This is a version of what he means by the event or occurrence that exceeds any recognition of it in the present. The excess is theorised best in its pathological sense in the philosophy of the sublime: 'This is probably a contradictory feeling. It is at the very least a sign, the question-mark itself, the way in which *it happens* is withheld and announced: *Is it happening?* The question can be modulated in any tone. But the mark of the question is "now", *now* like the feeling that nothing might happen: the nothingness now' (IN: 92). What Ramdani shows, though, is that the all-too-narrow aesthetics of the sublime does not do justice to the philosophy of the differend, in particular, in terms of a possible politics.

Where, after *The Differend*, Lyotard concentrates on the direct triggering of the feeling of the sublime as the sign of the differend or event, Ramdani returns with greater effect to the ideas of impossibility and radical difference at work in the philosophy of the sublime. What he shows is that the differend can be felt as much by a precise description of the conditions that give rise to the differend as by the aesthetics of the sublime. Thus painting, so valued by the later Lyotard, is not to be privileged in terms of the event and the politics of the differend: 'In the determination of pictorial art, the indeterminate, the "it happens" is the paint, the picture. The paint, the picture as occurrence or event, is not expressible, and it is to this that it has to witness' (IN: 93). Social and economic descriptions have as great a part to play.

The precision and truth of Lyotard's work on Algeria is paradoxical, at least when considered from a position overly accustomed to the association of truth with political progress. Lyotard's truth is critical but without providing us with a political teleology. He allows for a critique of the role of ideals in the description of the Algerian war of independence. But he does not provide us with a foundation for a revolutionary politics, because of the insistence that the truth of the conflict lies in an intractable difference. Ramdani asks how it was possible for a left-wing French intellectual to give a more precise analysis of the war than any other commentator, including Algerian thinkers and activists. His answer does not concentrate on Lyotard's two years spent teaching in Algeria (Constantine, 1952–4) and his love for the country (Lyotard 1989a: 38–9), but on the *Socialisme ou barbarie* group: 'In order to understand why a militant intellectual was able to show depth in the analysis of the Algerian war and how he was able to shed a sometimes unbearable light on the Algerian problem and the colonial question, we have to look at the history of the group he belonged to' (1989a: 24). This focus is justified but also contradictory in terms of Ramdani's use of the philosophy of the differend to frame the Algerian war: that philosophy and the work of *Socialisme ou barbarie* are no perfect match. It is worth noting that Lyotard does the same in his 1989 note of introduction to the Algerian texts (1989a: 33–9).

It is also important to note that Lyotard is often a poor commentator on his own work, if good commentary is to allow the text to retain some autonomy and its own temporality. He often reviews his life with his contemporary concerns and philosophy, revising the past in order either to fit it into the present thesis ('Algeria as differend and as intractable', Lyotard 1989a: 39) or to deflect incongruous past works ('*Libidinal Economy* is a metaphysical strike', DP: iii). Perhaps this anti-historical trait comes out most clearly in his pleasingly literary but historically restrictive autobiography *Peregrinations*. Iain Hamilton Grant's discussion of this book in his introduction to *Libidinal Economy* is particularly instructive and liberating on this issue (LE: xviii–xx). Against the tendency to privilege the author's auto-critique, Grant draws our attention to Lyotard's attacks on this kind of reading: 'But this is not a sanity trial – we are interested in writing, and writing, says Lyotard, is irresponsible' (xx). In a later commentary on his own work, Lyotard welcomes general rewriting, that is, on the part of any reader, as a necessary aspect of reading and writing (see his foreword to *The Lyotard Reader*). But the reworking of the essays on Algeria in terms of the differend imposes a restrictive tidiness that does not allow them their full critical contribution.

I do not want to deny the importance of connecting Lyotard's early and later work. That link allows for a strong presentation of the main characteristics of the work, most notably the philosophy of the event, the belief in absolute differences or the differend and the belief in intractableness. However, equally important is the development of Lyotard's work and the subtlety of each individual take on an issue or topic. So whilst agreeing that the differend allows for a clear and consistent explanation of Lyotard's work on Algeria, I want to stress that this work is also a stage on the way to the differend – and a particularly difficult one. I also want to stress that we have much to learn from the detail and the complex construction of all his essays, in the way they show the limits and difficulties of all the different analytical and philosophical tools and positions Lyotard is apt to blend as a modern-day essayist. In commenting on his articles for *Socialisme ou barbarie*, I want to insist on little-appreciated areas of his work, such as economics, political and social critique and the study of the limits of revolutionary critique.

ECONOMICS AND TERROR

Lyotard's interest in economics, in terms of a critical analysis of capitalism, is present throughout his work. It takes different forms, varying from a study in terms of a potential revolution in the work on Algeria, through a re-evaluation of basic economics in terms of desire in *Libidinal Economy* (LE: 155–240), to a critical concern with the relation of the capitalist language game to others through the medium of time in *The Differend* (TD: 173–81). The analytical flavour of Lyotard's work on capitalism is a constant in all these works; that is, he strives to understand, within a given philosophical framework, what makes capital powerful and what differentiates it from other pursuits. This framework is loosely Marxist, in *La Guerre des Algériens*, libidinal materialist in *Libidinal Economy* and linguistic in *The Differend*.

However, the political context for these analyses varies greatly from the early to the later work. Where the Algerian essays seek to allow for an understanding of capital in the context of a socialist revolution, the later works become much more sceptical about the role of revolution in framing the relation of economics to political action. Instead, they fall into greater or lesser degrees of working with, but also resisting, capital. The libidinal work concludes with complicity but also subversion, whilst the philosophy of the differend is concerned with resistance in the undermining of Ideas of reason, rather than with an overthrowing or a working through or the creation of a drift within capitalism.

The work on capitalism in *La Guerre des Algériens* has to be taken in two ways. First, it arrives at the practical impossibility of a socialist revolution in this particular case, but still within the search for a workers' revolution in different conditions. Second, it is a precursory sign of a theoretical flaw and practical failure of thinking in terms of revolution and beyond capitalism. Thus the essays allow us to understand why Lyotard ends up abandoning Marxism (like so many of his contemporaries), but without giving up on Marx as a philosophical resource. They also allow us to chart the emergence of various novel ways of thinking and feeling that come to replace the Marxist model. (The best essay showing the persistence of Lyotard's debt to Marx is his 'A Memorial to Marxism'.) In considering these issues it is essential to keep in mind the principal insight and main critical edge of *Socialisme ou barbarie*. This is to analyse the necessary relation between government and repressive bureaucracy both in capitalist states and in Stalinism, and as a corollary to other revolutionary movements, most notably Trotskyism.

This insight is essentially economic where Lyotard traces the operation of government and the attainment of economic growth in a broadly capitalist or Stalinist world to economic tools dependent upon bureaucratic management and the hegemony of a bureaucratic class. It is interesting to note that many years later Lyotard returns to the difficulties of this position between capitalism and Stalinism in his biography of André Malraux (SM: 179–202). However, this does not imply that *Socialisme ou barbarie* gave up on revolutionary aims. The powerful critique of the leading socialist movements of their day and the association drawn between these and capitalist bureaucracy is a stage on the way to revolution: 'I will then go on to consider which class will seize or has already seized control of the administrative organs that ensure exploitation, in order to ask what line the revolutionary movement ought to take, after we have defined the structure of power' (PW: 172).

Economic arguments run through most of the essays on Algeria. They allow Lyotard to define the operation and limits of revolutionary and counter-revolutionary power. In this sense, a well-known 'postmodern' paradox begins to emerge in the context of a modern conception of resolvable contradictions; one that prefigures his later analysis of the pervasiveness of capital and the way it exceeds individual or group control. Each time a class or nation is seen to hold power through economic means, it is also seen to be caught in a position where those means bar the way to resolving wider and, in the long term, more serious economic and social problems. In order to preserve a social and political dominance, a ruling class is forced to make economic choices that either deepen violent and unsustainable divides with other classes or hasten an economic decline with the same end result. Thus at this stage of his work, Lyotard's philosophy and politics are heavily indebted to Marx, even though the *Socialisme ou barbarie* group see their work as a departure from the more rigid political developments of Marxism and constantly seek to distance themselves from many of its strands (most notably Stalinism and the politics of the French communist party): 'We have to get rid of a certain kind of patronising Marxism: an ideology [the Algerian nationalist ideology] has no less *reality* (even and above all if it is *false*) than the objective relations to which this Marxism wants to reduce it' (PW: 199).

At this stage of Lyotard's work, what will later be analysed as a thoroughgoing paradox is only seen as a contradiction for a particular class or group. The contradiction must lead to the destruction or transformation of that class through revolution, but this turn of events also promises a proper resolution of the initial contradictions. By his late essays the idea of a postmodern economic 'system' that thrives on its contradictions and works with paradox takes over: 'Class struggles are elements, among others, that put up a resistance to the development of the system. But, as I said, the latter has need of such obstacles to improve its performance' (PF: 73). This 1993 essay, 'The Wall, the gulf, the system', begins with a remembrance of Lyotard's work with *Socialisme ou barbarie*, though the slack observation, memory and argument therein are on the verge of distasteful, in particular when one comes out of a reading of the earlier works. This contrast is a result of the different methods of the two periods. (The ironic style of the later works will be criticised with respect to its politics and incipient nihilism in Chapter 6.)

The first essay of *La Guerre des Algériens* analyses a contradiction in terms of imperialist repression and terror. French power is shown to depend upon the deliberate exclusion of Algerians from the means to economic development. This exclusion forces French economic policy into the mode of pillaging and exploitation as opposed to investment. The nature of French exploitation is defined by very weak capital investment and the appropriation of means of production in mining and agriculture to facilitate the export of raw materials to France (PW: 172–3). The consequences of this combination are the expropriation of Algerians from employment and the soil, with resulting poverty and famine, and very high levels of profit due to a high level of unemployment. The dishonestly circular reasoning for this form of exploitation is 'social stability' – later defined by Lyotard as the ability to continue exploiting Algeria at excessive rates of profitability.

France has an interest in keeping Algeria underdeveloped:

> In this sphere, the interest of the French cartels coincides with that of the colonists: both seek to maintain the north African economy in a pre-industrial state. If agriculture were industrialised, writes the director of agriculture to the government of Algeria, the fellahs would become industrial wage earners: 'Is it really in our interest to proletarianize future elements of the population, when social stability presumes an inverse development?'
>
> (PW: 172)

But this cynicism fuels the social revolution with a large population of disaffected and starving workers. It also fuels a national revolutionary fervour since wealth and power are seen to be almost exclusively French: 'The entire daily life of almost all Muslims is thus taken over and ground down by the handful of colonists: Maghrebi society is a totalitarian society, where exploitation presupposes terror' (PW: 174).

Economic policy is caught in a circle that cannot allow it to find an economic solution to the conflict. Once exploitation and a concomitant revolutionary fervour are set in motion it is no longer possible to seek to weaken that fervour by development, jobs and wealth. This is because the nature of order in Algeria has been set by an economic policy that demands repressive policing ('in the Maghreb the police perform an essential economic and social role'). It is impossible to break that relation without setting off an even greater push for revolution, since the lid is kept on that movement by keeping all forms of power in colonial hands. In these early essays we encounter a case of Lyotard's definition of totalitarianism and terror; terms to which he has always ascribed great philosophical and political importance. Terror in the Maghreb is not only the threat of random brutality and torture, but also the imposition of an alien culture and system as the only possible social conduit in terms of administration, education, culture and employment.

This defines the necessary relation between totalitarianism and terror. All aspects of Algerian society are colonised and run by colonials; hence the terror that seeps into anything that stands outside the colonial system through the threat of starvation and repressive exclusion. Algerians are terrorised into working within a system that cannot accept their traditions, claims to fair employment and to decent living conditions. This is the second strand of Lyotard's argument on the impossibility of economic reform. Economic exploitation leads to a revolutionary nationalist politics because France is identified with all the repressive aspects of Algerian society. The only *real* solution – Lyotard and *Socialisme ou barbarie* tend to make great play of this anti-idealistic economic and social realism – is then to achieve independence from France: 'Therefore the struggle situates itself immediately at the national level; it spontaneously seeks to suppress the apparatus of state terror where oppression takes on its most obvious shape and independence' (PW: 174).

More than twenty years later, by the time of Lyotard's *Just Gaming* and *The Differend*, terror and totalitarianism have been defined more generally. Terror is the imposition of a mode of expression that is inconsistent with what has to be expressed. Totalitarianism is the illegitimate grounding of universal moral and political judgements on exclusive views masquerading as judgements of fact. Geoffrey Bennington and Bill Readings explain this illegitimate extension of truth into value in different contexts, but they agree that therein lies Lyotard's key insight into terror and totalitarianism:

> The representable law, the prescriptive which claims to be grounded in either a description of the true nature of society, or of the will of the universal subject of humanity, or of the grand narrative of historical destiny, institutes terror in that it silences resistance by victimization: those who lie outside the law (since the law is the justice of non-metaphorical reality) are unreal and cannot speak.
>
> (Readings 1991: 112)

> Whereas the rational terror of the French revolution is in principle generalisable in the name of 'Reason' to the whole of humanity, Nazi 'terror' makes an exception and simply eliminates the rest: just as in the Athenian funeral oration decried by Socrates, where the slippage among the pronouns and sentence-instances allowed a move from 'they were good' to 'we are good', in so far as 'we are Athenians', so here Aryans recount to other Aryans the story of (all) good Aryans.
>
> (Bennington 1988: 151)

Readings insists on the concern with law and justice in the later Lyotard. He draws our attention to Lyotard's separation of justice from matters or fact and to the critique of law based on claims to final representation of matters of fact. This is also a critique of terror: 'terror is not incidental in Lyotard's account of politics: our entire understanding of politics . . . is terroristic insofar as the political theorist, the state, or society claims to determine what justice is, to derive political prescriptions in reference to a describable state of affairs' (Readings 1991: 113).

Bennington, on the other hand, stresses the terrorism of exclusive narratives of legitimation. Terror is to legitimise a state, people, law according to a story that excludes some of those to be acted upon from an original foundation. Lyotard often returns to this narration of legitimacy and beginnings (most famously, though not best, in his attack on grand narratives in *The Postmodern Condition*, 'the grand narrative has lost its credibility', 37). His favoured way of thinking this through is in terms of the function and legitimacy of the term 'we', as in the statement 'We know what reason is'. This 'we' is discussed best in terms of terror in the essay 'Universal history and cultural differences' in *The Lyotard Reader*: 'Terror is no longer exercised in the name of freedom, but in the name of "our" satisfaction, in the name of a satisfaction of a *we* which is definitely restricted to singularity' (316–17).

The shift from the early description of terror in terms of a particular case to the later general definition is instructive and important. In the former, specific economic arguments and descriptions of a social reality form the basis for the identification of terror and the argument about what form revolutionary political action must take. In the latter, a theory-independent economy and sociology grounds a general claim that also applies to econ-omic and sociological descriptions. Despite the links in terms of subject (terror) and political aim (to eliminate terror), the two approaches are fundamentally inconsistent at the level of theory. The later work rejects the privileged role given to descriptive sentences in the early work and turns against any objective appeal to reality. Instead, naming, showing and making truth-claims about something become one mode of speaking among many *untranslatable* modes:

> Moreover, when it is a question of reality, it must be understood that reality is not only at play in cognitive phrases linked up with nominatives and ostensives. Reality plays itself out in the three families that have just been named, but also in all the other families of phrases (which are nonetheless untranslatable into the first three as well as into one another).
>
> (TD: 55)

So when Lyotard describes real economic and social contradictions in the essays on Algeria he falls foul of the lessons learnt in the later work. There is no one reality to which any critic can appeal in making political predictions and in determining rights and wrongs.

Instead, reality is the site of irreconcilable differences or differends, including differences about matters of fact: 'Reality entails the differend' (TD: 55). Lyotard's work on Algeria is not therefore simply about a differend. It is a painful progress towards the differend through the failure of an appeal to the reality of resolvable contradictions. The first essay in *La Guerre des Algériens* deduces a socialist and nationalist revolution in Algeria. But this deduction already betrays doubts about the future of the revolution in the role of the new Algerian bourgeois and bureaucratic proprietors and power-brokers: 'In reality, there is no alternative to exploitation than socialism; in reality, the national-democratic struggle of the North African people contains within it the seeds of a new mode of exploitation' (PW: 174). These doubts grow and come to overwhelm the theoretical apparatus that gave rise to the original predictions. Lyotard moves from a theory about economic and social contradictions and how to resolve them, to a theory about why descriptive theories must always fail to capture the social reality they set out to analyse. This failure can be ascribed to irresolvable contradictions inherent in any social reality; that is, that it must involve different and untranslatable claims to truth.

It is important, though, not to fall into the trap of only reading Lyotard's work backwards. The early work also stands in judgement over the later scepticism. With the differend and the turn against objectivity Lyotard loses the specificity and the belief in revolutionary progress of the earlier work. The price of the critique of appeals to reality and objectivity is a move away from political action that promises social change on the basis of well-founded analyses and predictions. So the later work retains the affects and emotion of the earlier work, but it cannot offer a redress in the sense of the elimination of a wrong through a well-defined progressive political path. Again, despair and nihilism appear to haunt the later Lyotard in a way that seems utterly strange when we experience the force and conviction of the essays on Algeria: 'Lastly, it is important to understand and to make it understood that the only lasting solutions (the solutions that none in the struggle can provide) are class solutions, the first of these being the direct appropriation of the land by the peasantry' (PW: 178). Though none of the protagonists can yet provide a solution, there is still a belief in a solution. By the end of the work on Algeria this belief in the possibility of deducing solutions is on the wane.

ALGERIA AFTER INDEPENDENCE

After Algerian independence, in the essay 'Algeria evacuated', Lyotard asks two questions that lead ultimately to a sense of discouragement: 'Why was there no revolution in Algeria?' and 'How can there be a revolution in Algeria?' The answer to the first question is developed in terms of the capacity of different post-revolutionary classes and political parties to bring about revolution. He studies the way in which the bourgeoisie, the urban proletariat and the peasantry react to independence. This reaction is then used to explain the failure of political good will towards revolutionary aims; these are represented through the figure of the post-independence leader Ben Bella and his revolutionary programme presented in Tripoli on his release from prison. This section of 'Algeria evacuated' is omitted from its translation in *Political Writings* on the grounds that it concerns 'a detailed description of political manoeuvres' (339). This is a shame since it leaves the reader with the impression that the failure of the revolution is wholly a failure of classes rather than a failure of classes to bring enough political will to bear on what was a worthwhile, if far from perfect, political programme.

So it is not only a question of a political vacuum, but rather a lack of political impulse that leads to a corruption of political classes: 'When it became necessary to organise the political instrument necessary for the implementation [of the programme] conflict broke out' (1989a: 249); 'Truth is that in the absence of pressure from the masses, in an ideological vacuum and in organisational deficiency the fight for power became opportunistic' (1989a: 251). So it was not simply political corruption, nor simply the failure of revolutionary classes to rise spontaneously. It was the detachment of politics from revolutionary classes that led to the absence of revolution. Lyotard analyses this in terms of the bourgeoisie, urban workers and peasantry.

First, the bourgeoisie. According to Lyotard, the failure of the Algerian bourgeoisie is double. The first fault is inherent to any bourgeoisie; that is, to seek to defuse revolutionary forces in order to maintain its grip on property, political power and culture. The second fault, however, is characteristic of the North African bourgeoisie. It is to resist moves towards industrial development by concentrating capital in traditional forms such as land and property for rental income. Instead of investing towards greater industrial development – and thereby contributing to a future revolution through the creation of an urban proletariat – the North African bourgeoisie sticks to its traditions as a *rentier* class. This critique is a constant through all Lyotard's essays on Algeria, from some of the earliest such as 'The North African bourgeoisie' right up to the essays on post-revolutionary Algeria. At every turn, the bourgeoisie is seen to be reactive and backward-looking except for its role in nationalism: 'Bourguiba wants to give that leadership back to the Algerian bourgeoisie: it is true that the moment of French exhaustion, which will favour this draws near. But this little runt of a bourgeoisie, the outdated product of the period of direct administration, does not represent a social force' (PW: 186).

The French withdrawal from Algeria does not lead, therefore, to an investment in desperately needed factories and farm machinery, but to a speculative rush to acquire land:

> During the last years of the war, Algerian farmers and managers, profiting from the absence of the property owners and from the absence of control, pocketed the land revenues; lands, buildings and small firms were repurchased by the weak Algerian middle classes. Speculation allowed it to enlarge its nest egg pretty quickly.
>
> (PW: 304)

But that is all capital is for this bourgeoisie: a nest egg. It is not the opportunity to put capital to work, but rather a source of *rentier* income to be protected and extended in terms of property and not in terms of economic development through investment.

This is serious enough as an economic failing, but it becomes a political failing through a double corruption of the nascent state. The apparatus is affected intellectually and in terms of its *modus operandi*: 'The corruption of the civil servants went along with this enrichment of notables and businessmen. They sabotaged the purges and favoured the invasion of the administration by their cronies. The new bourgeoisie proliferated in the bosom of the state' (PW: 305). The speculative practice of the bourgeoisie bequeaths the state a destiny of corruption and underdevelopment. It also puts the state once again into the hands of France, since the new leaders are easily corrupted into preserving the economic interests of the old colonial power. French capitalism gives the state and its bourgeois bureaucrats funds in return for an extension of deals on the exploitation of raw materials: 'Thus imperialism found a new bridgehead in the country among the speculators in the administration' (305).

Worse still, the Algerian bourgeois are just as likely to move their liquid capital to 'safe' foreign shores at the first sign of revolutionary ferment, leaving the state doubly in hock to forces that wish to see a continuation of the pre-revolutionary economic situation (306). In Lyotard's eyes this is the ultimate betrayal of the revolutionary independence movement, because the movement was born of this very regime of exploitation and corruption. All that remains on the plus side of independence is the replacement of foreign oppressors by Algerians. This is no little achievement, but it is no revolution.

It would be wrong, though, to deduce a prejudiced view of the North African bourgeoisie as opposed to the 'Western bourgeois' from this critique. Lyotard's point is rather that in North Africa the bourgeoisie has not been allowed to develop into a class capable of development, investment and progressive political leadership because it has not itself been allowed to grow and develop due to its usurpation by colonials: 'The only bourgeoisie

21

in the strict and decisive sense (a bourgeoisie that possesses the means of production) was the European bourgeoisie . . .' (304). His arguments are economic and do not concern racial 'essences'. The Algerian bourgeoisie has not been allowed to develop away from economically outdated traditions governed by a mercantilism encouraged by the Koran. These ideas return – again much more lightly – in the 'The Wall, the gulf, the system' on the fall of the Eastern bloc and the Gulf war (PF: 79).

Second, the proletariat and peasantry. In the case of the urban proletariat and the peasantry Lyotard has to explain why they failed to provide continued impetus to the revolution once independence was achieved. How can the absence of these classes from the post-independence political scene be accounted for? These questions are particularly difficult, since stock answers such as 'living conditions were improved' and 'grievances were answered' are manifestly untrue: 'While the factions struggled for power, the phantom of unemployment and famine already haunted the people of the countryside and the cities' (PW: 294). They are also difficult since those classes showed great courage and made great sacrifices during the war of independence. Lyotard's reply is perhaps the most contentious but also characteristic aspect of his philosophy – regarding Algeria, but also much later. He separates the spontaneous uprising of masses against wrongs or for needs and any political theory that gives that spontaneity direction, at the time or even in terms of a later interpretation. Theory does not play a determining role in mass movements. Instead, the very notion of mass depends on reactions and desires that bring disparate groups together for the length of time it takes to move against a common abhorrence or towards a common good.

This division of desire and theoretical construct, allied to a conception of an original disparateness of society, becomes one of the most important aspects of Lyotard's work. It appears in the post-1968 essays collected in *Dérive à partir de Marx et Freud*. In turn, these essays anticipate *Libidinal Economy*: 'One can imagine any society as an ensemble of persons ruled by a system whose function would be to regulate the entry, the distribution, and the elimination of the *energy* that this ensemble spends in order to exist' (PW: 63). The same thoughts can also be found in Lyotard's extended study of discourse and art, *Discours, figure*: 'the event as disturbance always defies knowledge . . .' (22). So desires are channelled but, as in the case of Algeria, they can also erupt as events that come to disrupt an established system: 'However, the qualitative event occurs when the very forms through which energy is rendered circulable (the institutions, in the sense that I have given to the term) cease to be able to harness that energy – they become obsolete' (65).

In *Libidinal Economy*, Lyotard develops the earlier description into an opposition drawn between intensity (energy) and dispositions (organisation). There is an irreducible difference separating the energy behind social movements and the theories involved in understanding them or in giving political direction to them. Understanding and direction are necessary, but also insufficient. In the language of *Libidinal Economy*, intensity and difference are dissimulated within these dispositions, concealed but never fully captured: 'Let us be content to recognize in dissimulation all that we have been seeking, difference within identity, the chance event within the foresight of composition, passion within reason' (52).

The importance of the political event thought of in terms of feelings and desires also appears in Lyotard later work on the differend. It is developed from a reading of Kant found in the 1982 essay 'The Sign of history' and taken further in *The Differend* and Lyotard's fullest treatment of Kant, *L'Enthousiasme*. By this stage, he thinks through political events in terms of the sublime and, in shocking contrast to early work, the key affects are those of spectators. One of the distinguishing features of Lyotard's work on Algeria is his insistence on the decisive part to be played by Algerians as opposed to foreign sympathisers, including revolutionaries and workers. In the work on Kant, the opposite is the case: it is as if only the more detached feelings of outsiders offer a true insight into the events. The crux of the argument is that the significance of political events is indicated by the sublime feelings felt by spectators to the event. The sublime is a combination of two opposed feelings: the feeling that the imagination must provide a presentation of an idea of reason, such as the idea of an 'emancipated working humanity', and the feeling that it cannot do so (TD: 165–7). It is therefore a combination of expectation and frustration triggered by a historical event (in Kant's work, the French revolution).

What matters for the discussion of Algeria are the continuities and breaks with Lyotard's early work. He uses the Kantian theory of the sublime to further a thesis about the heterogeneity of linguistic practices, and by this he means to include all social events. In terms of the revolutionary aims of the work on Algeria, the most serious aspect of this move towards social heterogeneity, indicated by the feelings of spectators to a historical event, lies in the critique of Marxism put forward straight after the study of Kantian enthusiasm in *The Differend*. I shall return to this critique and to the reaction to *Socialisme et barbarie* found in *Libidinal Economy* in the last critical section of this chapter.

Notwithstanding later theoretical moves regarding radical social differences and heterogeneity, Lyotard's arguments concerning the inactivity of the proletariat and peasantry concentrate on the objective dissolution of masses. In 'Algeria evacuated' he ascribes the coherence of the masses involved in the war of revolution to a reaction against the impoverished and racist image of Algerians. This reaction is as much a fight against the tacit adoption of this image in Algerians as it is against French occupation and racism: 'The pursuit of independence consisted in delivering oneself from the colonial nightmare. It could not be more intense than during the

23

struggle, when the masses broke and trampled their own caricature under-foot' (PW: 302).

But this unity hides an original set of differences that show the notion of mass to be nothing without the singular desire that gave it consistency and strength: 'The composite character of what has been called the masses is a less momentary element. There are peasants, workers, the middle class, each group traversed by the conflict between generations, by a more or less strong adherence to traditional culture, by the nature of needs, by language' (PW: 301). This divisiveness runs through even the apparently most coherent class, the peasantry:

> Then class antagonisms are embroidered onto the particoloured costume that makes up the bled (hinterland), class antagonisms that are more or less distinct according to the degree of capitalist penetration into the countryside (it is dominant in the colonized flatlands), or according to the persistence of the Algerian feudal class (as in the high plain of the Constantinois or the Oranais), or according to the survival of tribal or village communities (in Kabylie, in the Aurès).
>
> (301)

Lyotard and *Socialisme ou barbarie*'s realism comes to the fore here (and it is interesting to note that much of the close analysis owes a great deal to the sociological studies of Algeria by the now equally influential thinker Pierre Bourdieu; see *Sociologie de l'Algérie*). This objectivity has three critical strands for any reflection on the post-independence role of the masses:

1   Lyotard explains their unity and revolutionary fervour through the desire to destroy a self-image and not through a political class-consciousness; it is thus an argument about feelings of revulsion and deliverance rather than about consciousness and understanding.
2   No single characteristic of a class or mass is allowed to dominate in its definition or in any argument for its continuous identity. There is an awareness that each class is an amalgam of characteristics, each of which can pull it apart given the right situation.
3   Classes are seen to overlap through these characteristics and through complex economic and social interrelationships. There is no simple economic or social logic that allows for theoretical accounts of the play of one class with another.

These points are used by Lyotard, often in combination, in order to explain different failures in the revolutionary movement. For example, when considering the counter-argument that the peasantry can be organised into a revolutionary mass by land claims, he shows how those claims do not in reality lead to cohesiveness. He divides the peasants by geographical region, in order to show that the nature of their claims has to be different: 'To understand [the post-independence hiatus], one can turn to the diversity of regional situations and the limits they impose on social consciousness' (PW: 308). In regions where land is scarce and where there is little land to be re-distributed among many small-holders there is very little pressure towards land-reforms (308). On the other hand, where there are labourers rather than small-holders, the obstacle lies in tradition and attitude. The historical relation between owner and labourer is partly extra-financial, in the form of a duty on the part of the former to pay the latter in kind and to ensure subsistence even in times of great scarcity. This means that 'social relations are not the product of a logic of interest, which is born only with mercan-tilism, but of an ethics governed by traditional rights and duties' (309).

This form of argument against theoretical unity and political logic through an appeal to a complex, fluid and emotionally driven reality recurs throughout Lyotard's essays on Algeria, though the point here is not that he proved to be accurate in the time-span of the essays or that it provides a useful starting-point for a study extending into the terrible present. Rather, it is to assess the philosophical potential and flaws of the approach, first in terms of Lyotard's criticisms of the left and right on Algeria, then in terms of the interaction between his own works.

CRITICAL ATTACKS ON THE LEFT AND THE RIGHT

Lyotard's essays on Algeria are not solely concerned with an Algerian revolution and war of independence. They study the metropolitan dimen-sion of that struggle in two connected ways. How do actions in France affect Algeria? What do those actions tell us about the political situation in France? Broadly, the answers to these questions are as follows:

1   There is an absence of solidarity and concern for the Algerian masses on the part of the French working classes.
2   There is an absence of revolutionary political desires among the French, even in the context of a revolution in France.
3   The French left wing is not capable of responding to the Algerian situation as revolutionary *and* as a struggle for independence. That is, there is a belief that the revolution must take place in the context of an international socialism. Independence is then not a step towards revolution; quite the contrary.
4   The French left wing has not taken on board the lack of desire for revolution in France.
5   The French right wing is not capable of resolving the economic contradictions that give rise to revolutionary desires in Algeria.

The explanation for points 3 and 5 has been given above. The necessary terroristic control of all Algerian institutions by the French is a final barrier to the resolution of economic and social problems while Algeria is under French control: 'The absurdity of the military task in Algeria is that it wants at the same time to manage Algeria with the Algerians and without them (not to say against them)' (PW: 266). There is a double hurdle to cross in any social and economic reform in Algeria: power would have to be given over to workers *and* to Algerian workers.

But this does not explain the depoliticisation of French workers: 'Yet, with the exception of Algeria (where such a political life, even if it is in decline, appeared in January among the Europeans, and where it manifests itself every day without fail in the shape of the armed activity of the Algerians themselves), France is politically dead' (252). Why has politics, or a certain kind of modern politics, come to die in France in the late fifties, early sixties? Is it helpful to think of Lyotard's later work on the post-modern as an attempt to explain this death? Now these are dangerous questions. They direct us to the most superficial and well known of his works, *The Postmodern Condition*, and to the most simple and blunt explanation of the shift into a postmodern politics. But his work has little to do with simply charting the death of modern politics and everything to do with the attempt to create new ways of thinking the political and to rekindle politics under another guise.

The points that he gives in explanation for depoliticisation are useful because they provide new challenges for a philosophy that does not want to see political desire seep away. 'The State and Politics in the France of 1960' puts them forward in a sketch (the original version numbers each point; these disappear in the English translation):

1   Economic growth brought about by greater productivity is accompanied by a change in the relation of worker to work and work to capital. There is even greater worker alienation in work because the tasks they have to perform as dictated by the means to achieve greater productivity have no interest or real meaning for them. This also means that the relation between particular tasks and amounts of pay has become arbitrary.

2   In 'return' for this alienation workers receive more pay in terms of purchasing power. But this does not mean greater freedom, or that workers have become equal to owners. The corollary to increased purchasing power is greater outside control over what is purchased. Workers' needs are tailored to what is produced; and what is produced is tailored to those needs: 'The needs we feel are less and less our needs, more and more anonymous needs, and the infallible symptom of this alienation is that the satisfaction of needs does not procure a real pleasure' (271).

3 Economic expansion has led to a homogenisation of French life. Those involved in modes of life that had escaped this alienation, such as farmers, shopkeepers and artisans, now fall prey to it.
4 Not only work, but all other traditional human relations such as family life and life in neighbourhoods have broken down. This leads to a more testing individual lifestyle, at the same time more difficult but also more experimental. So a global sense of society disappears with the sense that it is possible to reconstitute that sense.
5 This loss of sense is most acute among the young. Their depoliticisation is the form taken by a more general separation from social values.

Lyotard connects all these points to a single property of capitalism, that is, the capacity to incorporate opposition and critique into the system. The depoliticisation of the French proletariat and youth comes from the way in which their revolutionary political activities are assimilated into capitalism. This assimilation places any struggle 'in the past tense' and places political activists 'in the passive mood'. It is not only the ideas and demands of the proletariat that are assimilated in this way but also the forms of struggle. The union becomes a means of management, and representatives of the proletariat become part of the bureaucratic management class:

It is thus proletarian political life itself that is alienated, that is displaced from its own class in hybrid organisms (in that their genesis is worker and their function is bureaucratic, that is seized by the ruling class). The very idea of a global political project is immediately neutralized in the workers' own heads. Incredulity, lassitude, and irony keep an exploited class in step much more effectively than open violence.

(275)

From many points of view this situation has much to commend it in terms of social stability, better working conditions and increased wealth – Lyotard is well aware of this. But it still needs a revolutionary critique because of the erosion of activities and ideals involved in the passivity induced by the shift into bureaucratic capitalism. A loss of 'direction, sense and values' must be remedied by revolutionary activity. But this cannot be the traditional activity of the left, 'minuscule in relation to the real dimensions of the crisis'. This is why Lyotard's philosophy moves towards postmodernity and the libidinal: he can neither work within a system whose capacity to assimilate difference neutralises its value and intensity, nor work to overthrow the system according to traditional revolutionary politics, since this has fed the very cause of the crisis.

THE LIBIDINAL DRIFT AWAY FROM CRITIQUE

Why does Lyotard's method change after *La Guerre des Algériens*? What does that change indicate in terms of problems with that method? What can we learn from his essays on Algeria, in terms of contemporary politics and philosophy? As I hope to have shown, any lesson cannot be solely that the Algerian war must be considered in terms of a differend. Matters are much more complex than that, not only in terms of the different economic and social groups and desires involved, but also in terms of the methodology employed. Irrespective of what Lyotard says in his reinterpretation of former selves, the method of *La Guerre des Algériens* is not that of *The Differend*. More to the point, I want to argue that this method and its results bequeath more to and are given more from *Libidinal Economy* than *The Differend*. Finally, it is essential to insist again that Lyotard's early work is not only to be judged from the standpoint of the later work. Cutting critical points can also be made against the later work from the political activity of the essays on Algeria.

In *La Guerre des Algériens*, Lyotard's method depends upon: (a) an articulation of the social field into classes; (b) an explanation of the logical relations between those classes in terms of objective economic and sociological relations; (c) a political aim of revolution brought about by the spontaneous rising of masses informed, but not led, by critical studies such as those put forward in *Socialisme ou barbarie*. The emphasis, then, is on critique rather than political organisation and leadership (naturally, given that the main critical focus of the *Socialisme ou barbarie* group is bureaucracy). The focus is on class rather than individuals or political parties. It is on revolution, rather than on evolution.

By *Libidinal Economy* the three strands of this method are undone and replaced. This is not a matter of whimsy or chance, but a reaction to inaccuracy and a resulting painful failure in the early work: '. . . so that [our readers] consider our flight into libidinal economy for what it is, the solution to a long pain and the breach out of a difficult impasse' (LE: 117). Pages 113 to 154 of *Libidinal Economy* are a cruel dissection of the desires behind the theory and the 'reality' of Lyotard's essays on Algeria (and related works by others). This does not mean that the later work is only a metaphysical 'blow'. If it is metaphysical, it is to be read from the thesis that there is nothing outside metaphysics. Thus 'reality' and 'truth' only take on their full philosophical force from the Nietzschean perspective of the desires at work within the creation of *a* reality and *a* truth – that is, one among many.

The comments on Algeria in *Libidinal Economy* are searing, as raw today as they must have been in less cynical and knowing days: 'hang on tight and spit on me . . .' (111). They are written to trigger (to bury) desires deep in the reader. But it is possible to read off a theoretical position that dissimulates that emotion:

1   Actions are understood better in terms of physical and unconscious desires and not in terms of abstract ideas: 'There is no libidinal dignity, nor libidinal fraternity, there are libidinal contacts without communication (for want of a "message"). This is why, amongst individuals participating in the same struggle, there may exist the most profound miscomprehension, even if they are situated in the same social and economic bracket' (113).

2   Libidinal investment in an action is unstable and impermanent. It changes and dies in a practice that it energises and gives direction to. So a social identity does not only define the investment; the opposite is also the case: 'Now these disparities, which are heterogeneities of investment in the erotic or deadly fluxes, are of course found within any social "movement" whatsoever, whether minute, on the scale of a factory, or immense, when it spreads to a whole country or continent' (113–14).

3   Any situation is prey to an open set of heterogeneous desires. Or, in the words of *Libidinal Economy*, every political economy is libidinal and there are no primitive societies (122–7).

4   Given these three points, Lyotard goes on to claim capitalism as the system best suited to handling – that is, channelling and exploiting – desires in their unpredictability and heterogeneity. Capitalism adapts to new desires and can regulate heterogeneity through monetary equivalences: 'Capitalism includes, on the contrary, in the name of increased accumulation, growth, development, etc., *a dispositif [disposition/set-up] of the regulation of conquest*, a *dispositif* of permanent conquest. The speciality of this *dispositif* lies in a certain use of currency, which is a game with time' (154).

5   So there is no realm outside the potential of capitalism. There is no revolutionary state or primitive society that is not open to a capitalist exploitation of desire and heterogeneity: '. . . there is no external reference, even if immanent, from which the separation of what belongs to capital (or political economy) and what belongs to subversion (or libidinal economy), can always be made, and cleanly; where desire would be clearly legible, where its proper economy would not be scrambled' (108).

Once applied to the methodology of the essays on Algeria, these points lead away from classes and to desires. They lead away from an impossible privileging of a class, or even a desire, to the question of what the proper philosophical reaction should be to the heterogeneity and instability of desires. They lead away from a belief in a revolutionary state, and even more, from a hope for a post-revolutionary state. Instead, the central question becomes how best to be revolutionary with capitalism.

To some, including the early Lyotard, these conclusions are difficult and revolting. But, in *Libidinal Economy*, he takes a perverse pleasure in avoiding any sweetening of the pill by adopting an affirmative style free of regret and nostalgia. This also marks the great difference between *Libidinal Economy* and *Dérive à partir de Marx et Freud*: the latter shares many of the insights of the former, notably concerning the end of critique, but it does not make the leap into affirmation. But to fail to make this leap is inconsistent.

There is an amusing, but to some degree also quite serious, discussion between Lyotard and Derrida on their differing attitudes to nostalgia in the collection of *Les fins de l'homme: à partir du travail de Jacques Derrida* (310–15). This is reproduced in part in *The Lyotard Reader*: 'Then, I [Lyotard] would be indiscreet if I were to intervene in your nostalgia just as you were indiscreet to intervene in my resoluteness' (388). The humorous tone of this exchange masks a subtle but important difference between the two thinkers in their way of living with the weight of the past, including a shared concern with Algeria. Where Derrida works his deconstruction within past methods and philosophies in the dimensions they share with the present, Lyotard searches for a clean methodological break.

So when Derrida says, amid much laughter, that 'it was more than an idiosyncratic comparison . . .: in the resolute break with nostalgia, there is a psychoanalytic–Hegelian logic, a rigid relation, not very well regulated; there is perhaps more nostalgia in you than in me' (388–9), he is not only making a good joke at Lyotard's expense, given his well-known anti-Hegelianism; he is also pointing out that a resolute effort to escape the past is as burdened with nostalgia as the effort to live within the past. Negation cannot escape what it negates. But this is in turn unfair to Lyotard's analysis of desire, though maybe not to his later philosophy of the differend. Lyotard's work on desire is precisely an effort to show that it is futile to want to escape or negate desire and desires.

Nowhere are the pain of the lessons learnt by Lyotard and his methodological resoluteness more clear than in the references to Algeria and *Socialisme ou barbarie* in *Libidinal Economy*. In a direct line to the arguments in 'Algeria evacuated', he gives a libidinal study of the desires at work in the Algerian war of independence. This time the post-independence disaffection, bourgeois corruption and disintegration of the masses are not studied in terms of social and economic conditions, but in terms of the impermanence of desire: 'There are libidinal positions, tenable or not, there are positions invested which are immediately disinvested, the energy passing onto other pieces of the great puzzle, inventing new fragments and new modalities of *jouissance*, that is to say of intensification' (113). The use of the term 'jouissance', or enjoyment in a strong possessive and also sexual sense, indicates the indifference of desire. It can be taken through anything and does not fit judgements of good and bad or the guidance of conscience. Desire knows no norm or direction: it can bring political actors together, but also pull them apart: 'This is why, amongst individuals participating in the same struggle, there may exist the most profound miscomprehension, even if they are situated in the same social and economic bracket' (113).

As the desire to escape certain desires once and for all, the Algerian revolution had to fail, according to the later Lyotard. The desires to accumulate as a *rentier*, or to betray the revolution in self-serving compromise and calculation, or to further terror in the enjoyment of murder, are always latent. No revolution can banish them ('perhaps his desire still remained in the grip of the punitive relation he meant to abandon . . . already nourishing contempt for the body and exalting words as negotiation demands'). This is also true of other attempts to renew Marxism through the definition of novel zones that can be and must be allowed to grow outside the hegemony of capital.

In *Libidinal Economy*, Lyotard attacks the early Baudrillard's definition of primitive forms of exchange that come before capital in *The Mirror of Production* and *For a Critique of the Political Economy of the Sign* (LE: 103–8). Of course, Baudrillard was then to renounce his own work and drift into hyperreality (*America*; *Simulations*). Lyotard also puts forward a vitriolic attack on his former associate from *Socialisme ou barbarie*, Cornelius Castoriadis, for his attempt to define a generalised 'spontaneity and creativity' as a privileged realm in *La Société bureaucratique Vol I, II* and *L'Expérience du mouvement ouvrier Vol I, II* (LE: 116–19). Lyotard's objection is that there can be no general theory that can define such a realm. So there can be no simple revolution in favour of it. To continue to make this claim is to misunderstand the capacity of desire to escape and undo our theoretical categories of creativity and spontaneity:

> . . . we had to say. let's also eliminate the idea of revolution . . ., the idea of a reversal of position in the sphere of political economic power and therefore the idea of maintaining this or that sphere, or even, to be fairer to Castoriadis, the idea of a generalised reversal of position in *all* spheres; . . . for [this thought] was once again a wall, the same wall of the same impasse . . .
>
> (LE: 118)

But this does not free libidinal economy from the questions posed by the earlier Lyotard: What are we to make of our revolutionary desires? They exist, as do pain and terror. What, then, should we do to live with or live up to the desires, or to escape them? It could never be enough simply to proclaim the end of revolution, since all the commentary on Algeria in *Libidinal Economy* points towards revolutionary desires that have been forbidden a certain type of outlet according to a certain type of critical theory. Among the most pressing questions to be answered in the re-evaluation of Lyotard's libidinal work are the following: Does his work on

31

desire and capital commit him to a simple betrayal of his early revolutionary work? Can he still fight on the side of those who suffer terror, as he sought to do so tenaciously in the essays on Algeria?

THE SILENCING OF CRITIQUE

After a close study of Kant, *The Differend* ends with a set of aphorisms on capital. Numbers 236 to 239 are of particular interest to a critical reading of *La Guerre des Algériens*, since they argue against the capacity of a certain version of Marxism to resist the hegemony of capital. Again, some Marxist analyses and impulses continue with the philosophy of the different: '. . . the silent feeling that signals a differend remains to be listened to . . . This is the way in which Marxism has not come to an end, as the feeling of the differend.' However, despite these claims to continuity, the work on Marx in the differend develops a set of critical points against the earlier methods:

1   A wrong is not expressed through the description of specific social and economic practices and structures, but through the 'silent feeling that signals a differend'.
2   The 'solidary enthusiasm' that accompanies the silent feeling is not a legitimate basis for the deduction of an ideal 'revolutionary subject'.
3   This ideal is not evidence for a 'real political organisation of the real working class'.

So, like the work on Algeria in *Libidinal Economy*, the philosophy of the differend tries to explain the absence or transience of revolutionary masses charted in 'Algeria evacuated'. The methodology and political aims are very different; now Lyotard replaces both the description of relations between classes and descriptions in terms of desires with a critique of the possibility of relating real entities with Ideas of reason:

> The party is constrained to mistake the proletariat – a referent of the dialectical genre (in the Kantian sense), namely, the ideal object (and perhaps subject) of the Idea of emancipated working humanity – for the real working classes, the multiple referents of 'positive' cognitive phrases.
>
> (TD: 172)

We have seen this argument on the incommensurability of cognitive and other phrases at work earlier in the discussion of terror. It marks a theoretical and political demotion of accurate critical description in favour of the indicative feeling of the sublime. We have seen, too, that the nature of this feeling is a constitutive part of the argument for incommensurability. It also marks the shift into a politics of testimony, where we look for ways of expressing the differend indicated by our feelings, as opposed to a politics of revolution, where critique and political activism encourage the elimination of the differend.

The crux of this argument lies in the statement that this elimination is impossible: 'The repressed differend returns within the workers' movement, especially in the form of recurrent conflicts over the question of organisation . . .' (TD: 172). It is this impossibility that will be questioned most strongly in Chapter 5 on judgement and *The Differend*. Still, prior to any decision on validity, it is important to see what has been lost in Lyotard's drift away from revolution: the belief in the revolutionary role of objective critique against the inequities of capitalism. His work on Algeria is at the same time a step on the way to this loss and its indictment for disaffection.

3

LIBIDINAL ECONOMY AND NIHILISM

FOR A REVALUATION OF LIBIDINAL ECONOMY

> There is no intensity without a cry and without a labyrinth. The force which strikes a given surface of the great skin (that is to say which invents it) exhausts its surroundings by making it scream, and opens the maze of its flows. If infidelity makes the infidel cry as it does the man or woman to whom it is related, it is because their bodies, fragments of bodies, never cease haunting the areas surrounding the points on which force beats down. Your body itself, unfaithful one, is jealous of the intensities which your infidelity brings it, it too cries from the energy taken from it, and if it cries at the same time as your lover, it is because they belong to the same pulsional surroundings.
>
> (LE: 41)

Beautiful and exciting or obscure and distasteful? Is *Libidinal Economy* really a book of political philosophy? If it is, is it a book of responsible philosophy, dedicated to the true and the good? Or is it what we commonly dismiss as metaphysics: a set of classical or pseudo-scientific distinctions (energy–structure, desires–society, intense–weak) adopted uncritically as if true for eternity and wrapped up in rhetoric in order to give false political and moral power to the author? Metaphysics, in this sense, is the last refuge from the scrutiny of empirical research, the rectitude of established moral values and the discipline of logic. It should be our duty to ignore or pour scorn on this book, along with the two collections of essays related to it, *Dérive à partir de Marx et Freud* and *Des Dispositifs pulsionnels*. They seem to belong to an age of unreason characterised by the political disappointments of traditional revolutionary politics and the headiness of May 1968 (see *La Pensée 68* by Luc Ferry and Alain Renault).

So a few thinkers went that step too far: into anarchism, into the advocacy of desire free of control and social restraint, into obscure style and away from clarity and scholarliness. It is easy to understand their motives and the gain and pleasures that were theirs on the back of a *succès de scandale*. But it would be wrong for us to perpetuate that success. After the late sixties and the early seventies came dark years of terrorism and dissoluteness, where the degeneracy and disaffection of youth could be traced back to the false depth of the post-1968 'thinkers'. If any book merits to be forgotten or easily trashed as a paradigm of the misuse of philosophy, it must be *Libidinal Economy*.

But this reaction deserves its arguments more than Lyotard's work. *Libidinal Economy* is a rewarding book, rich in insight and experiment, but also and more covertly in experience and rigorous thought. It introduces new concepts into politics and philosophy. It does so deceptively: where there appears to be shoddy interpretation, there is often careful thought and preparation; where there appears to be mere opinion and posturing, there is an effort to design a political position in the light of modern difficulties and impossibilities; where there appears to be rhetoric, there is in fact an attempt to overcome the disabling aspects of the poststructuralist critique of traditional philosophy. It would be more accurate to say that Lyotard's libidinal work comes 'after and with' the critique of metaphysics and not simply as metaphysics. It comes after and with Marx, and the desire for liberating political action. It comes after and with truth, in the sense of seeking to create new truths for a situation that reveals the fragility and rigidity of established ones. *Libidinal Economy* is not a work of anti-philosophy, then, but of new philosophy, though it is not new in the reactionary sense of the *nouveaux philosophes*, whose self-serving efforts to market a reactionary and superficial set of intellectual values was powerfully criticised by Lyotard in *Tombeau de l'intellectuel* and *Instructions païennes*:

> There ought no longer to be 'intellectuals', and if there are any, it is because they are blind to this new fact in Western history since the eighteenth century: there is no universal subject-victim, appearing in reality, in whose name thought could draw up an indictment that would be at the same time a 'conception of the world' (look for names).
>
> (PW: 6–7)

The articles in *Tombeau de l'intellectuel* can be seen as a paradoxical response to Peter Dews's programme for the renewal of the left, put forward in his 'The "New philosophers" and the end of leftism' after a precise and variegated account of the relation of the *nouveaux philosophes* to post-1968 thought and to the left: 'We need to know how the unity of struggles, no longer pre-given by an inclusive primacy of class, can itself become a purpose of struggle' (Dews 1985: 384). Lyotard's answer is that this unity is precisely in the testimony of radical disunity as resistance to capital, as opposed to a profession that 'sells a product or a service that can be defined by its use, and hence can in principle be assessed' (PW: 12). The earlier *Instructions païennes* is a satirical attack on the way the *nouveaux philosophes* adopt their philosophies and publishing strategies to satisfy and eventually to corner markets: 'Behind the men of Clavel and co. [the *nouveaux philosophes*], the real novelty is the customs officer of theoretical discourses, narrative-as-money' (75).

The *nouveaux philosophes* have indeed taken on a function of policeman and conscience in the French media. Their position is loosely liberal democrat and rabidly anti-Marxist, anti-Heideggerian, anti-Nietzschean and anti-Hegelian (all said to have been compromised in the horrors of the twentieth century). They follow and then attempt to lead moral positions on the media issues of the day. Lyotard explains this moral and political authority in terms of the repetition of their views (X comments on Y who comments on Z and so on), allied to their common closeness to set 'acceptable' stock opinions and to the lack of real challenge to the aspect of capitalism as fixed power that encourages the exchange of the same (74–82).

The much more radical sense of 'new' searched for in all of Lyotard's works is that of a thought experimenting with ways of measuring up to contemporary conditions and events.These occurrences change the shape of things and render forms of thought obsolete and reactionary. But more than this, his philosophy seeks to open the way for actions in art, politics and philosophy that are consistent with the unpredictability and as yet unexpressed value of these events. This is how Bill Readings accounts for the continuity of Lyotard's works on the political in his subtle introduction to Lyotard's *Political Writings*: 'The possibility of politics lies in actions and desires that are sensible only as heard silences, traces of radical dissensus within modes and structures of political representation, social communication, or economic accounting' (xxv).

I believe that, like Mohammed Ramdani in the case of Lyotard's essays on Algeria, Readings gives too much methodological weight to the differend and to dissensus in applying the later methodology to earlier works: 'The obligation to remain alert to and respectful of voices that we cannot hear clearly cannot be lifted. That is the condition of politics, of the struggle to handle differends justly' (xxvi). Though sensitivity to events and opposition to established truths are present in all Lyotard's works, the earlier essays do not depend on this notion of silent differences. On the contrary, the method of the essays on Algeria is to describe real conditions as accurately as possible in order to reveal contradictions that can be overcome. It is a methodology that presupposes a real struggle between forces, where one is in the wrong and needs to be overpowered. There is no question of a necessity to lend an ear to some inexpressible other at work behind all differences; this comes later, in line with failures and disappointments in the early work, but also in line with a new sense of justice. As I hope to have shown in the previous chapter, in the essays on Algeria, Lyotard is still something of the modernist he is said to oppose: 'Lyotard's displacement of modernity is an insistence that these differences are not accidentally but structurally repressed by the modernist drive to transparency in representation, communication, and accounting, by the dream of self-autonomy' (xxv).

This is not merely a quibble over the reasons Lyotard gives for taking action in the face of an injustice and a differend. The import of these reasons comes out most strongly in the question of how to act. If it is indeed the case that a difference is irresolvable and that therein lies its value as a sign, then we are pushed into a politics of endless testimony ('Here is a differend that shows again that some differences cannot be resolved or presented in a final form'). If, on the other hand, there are differences that have not yet been resolved because we have not yet understood them, then we are pushed into a politics of accurate description with a view to go beyond the difference.

There is no doubt, though, that Readings is right in his analysis of the later philosophy of the differend. For example, Lyotard's argument against the *nouveaux philosophes* or 'intellectuals' is not only that they fail to understand the contemporary relation between markets and creative thought, but also that they must perpetuate this misunderstanding because they do not live with the necessity of the differend. Thus intellectuals forget or choose to forget that by asking for resolutions they are playing into the hands of a system that thrives on producing results for the sake of economic growth: 'Success in the management of culture is determined in principle in terms of results, in terms of changes in the behaviour of addressees that are judged to be positive' (PW: 4). Instead, the genuine artist, writer or philosopher experiments beyond recognised addressees, accepted criteria of judgement and well-defined disciplines.

This experimentation is not defined positively in 'Tomb of the intellectual', a response to the French politician Max Gallo's demand in the early eighties that intellectuals come to the aid of the incoming socialist government. Lyotard refuses to come on side. In his answer, he is concerned with separating creative activities from a responsibility towards the good management of capitalist societies (as he is in the related essays 'For a cultural nonpolicy', 'The Differend', 'Intellectual fashions' and 'A svelte appendix to the postmodern condition'). The positive definition given at this stage to Lyotard's ever-present defence of a revolutionary avant-garde is that they do not forget 'that politics is only business and culture is only tradition unless both of them are worked over by a sense of the differend . . .' (TD: 10).

37

Defined according to the opposition between intellectuals and avant-garde thinkers, this differend cannot become a result in a capitalist system. It cannot be resolved for the benefit of the system as a whole as if it were an obstacle to the smooth running of a machine, or to a more profitable circulation of capital, or to a gain of time in terms of production. So, by *The Differend*, the avant-garde is associated with absolute difference as the final form of resistance to capital: 'The only insurmountable obstacle that the hegemony of the economic genre comes up against is the heterogeneity of phrase regimen and of genres of discourse . . . The obstacle does not depend upon the "will" of human beings in one sense or another, but upon the differend. The differend is reborn from the very resolutions of supposed litigations' (TD: 181).

But this is not the case in the work on Algeria. There, the desire for revolution and for resolution remains, albeit in a fragile state. The outcome of this fragility is made clear in aphorism 262 of *The Differend*. The aphorism, placed right before the one quoted above, can be read as a regretful account of the difference between the politics of the differend and the politics of revolution in Algeria: 'The resistance of communities banded around their names and their narratives is counted on to stand in the way of capital's hegemony. This is a mistake. First of all this resistance fosters this hegemony as much as it counters it. Then, it puts off the Idea of a cosmopolitan history and generates the fear falling back onto legitimation through tradition' (TD: 181). The conclusion to the aphorism is a bitter, though perhaps not a justified condemnation of an earlier Lyotard: 'Proud struggles for independence end in young reactionary States.'

However, what I want to show in this chapter is that the contrast between *The Differend* and the Algerian essays also holds true for *Libidinal Economy*, but for different methodological and political reasons. I do not want to go against the general flow of interpretation that sees a continuity of concerns through Lyotard's philosophy, in particular in terms of a philosophy of the event (Bennington 1988; Readings 1991; Williams 1998). Rather, I want to show that this concern can be handled through radically different methodologies and hence radically different politics. In particular, in terms of the use of events to resist the hegemony of capital, *Libidinal Economy* defends a method dependent upon an unavoidable intermingling and interdependence of events and systems. This in turn leads to a politics of a working within *and against* capital, as opposed to a straightforward attempt to overthrow or resist. First, dissimulation, the central concept of interdependence and intermingling, but also of subversion from within, will be explained and analysed. This will allow for a study of the style and method of *Libidinal Economy*. Then an interpretation of Lyotard's libidinal politics will be developed in parallel with the study of the greatest problem to beset that philosophy: nihilism. The question of nihilism will be approached through Deleuze, Heidegger and Nietzsche.

STYLE AND ARGUMENTS

> . . . there is nothing the libido lacks in reality, nor does it lack
> regions to invest, the slender and very dark finger on her left
> hand which, in a conversation, the young woman, anxious
> because she is afraid of what she believes to be your erudition,
> passes over her eyebrow, while in her hand she pulls at a
> cigarette – here is a real region to invest, one can die for it, one
> can give all one's organicity, one's ordered body . . . for this
> finger which is like an engraver's stylus and the whole orbital
> space, cranial, vaginal, that it engenders around the eye.
>
> (LE: 4)

Libidinal Economy is written in a cinematic and surreal style. It unfolds at
speeds that vary impossibly, often in the course of a single trademark –
overstretched sentence. It shifts scale violently, panning from a mundane
description to metaphysical hyperbole and on to glimpses of pure theory in
too short a time for bearings to be taken. It releases the unconscious into a
philosophical discourse through familiar tropes, such as fleshy folds and
spreads, and through destabilising images and claims, too much or too far.
Suggestive, unsteadying topics and connections are created in an apparently
disordered and brutal manner. Sex and money, love and jealousy, philosophical theory and religion, linguistics and metaphysics burst into one
another in a heart-stopping manner. Just as an argument or narrative begins
to take shape and draw one in, something else, often something uncomfortable, breaks the flow and desecrates the purity of any burgeoning idea.

For example, begin to think that the key to Lyotard's thought lies in
Leibnizian incompossibility; this libidinal account of incompossibility in sex
destabilises the thesis:

> Virginensis is a cry forced out by all this at once, a cry made of
> several incompossible cries: she opens up, he takes me, she resists,
> he squeezes, she gets loose, he starts and stops, she obeys and
> commands, this could happen, happen impossibly, supplication and
> order, oh the most powerful thing of all flowing through them, do
> what desire desires, be its slave, connect, I give you a name.
>
> (LE: 8)

Or begin to draw up a straightforward critical dismissal, something like
'Lyotard's philosophy depends on a binary relation between desire and its
suppression, with an illegitimate valuation of desire through theory – let's
deconstruct.' Then this sneering denial makes your work that little bit

harder: 'We do not speak as the liberators of desire: idiots with their little fraternities, their Fourieresque fantasies, their policyholders' expectations over the libido' (42). Or even deduce from all the noise and confusion that this is an anarchic and violent work consistent with a terroristic or marginal politics, then puzzle over these concluding lines: 'We need not leave the place where we are, we need not be ashamed to speak in a "state-funded" university, write, get published, go commercial, love a woman, a man, and live together with them; there is no good place, the private universities are like the others, savage publications like civilized ones, and no love can prevail over jealousy' (262).

This does not mean that *Libidinal Economy* escapes from traditional philosophical and political questions concerning the true and the good. On the contrary, the book has an important contribution to make to the way in which we ask those questions and to the expectations we may have about possible answers. Those who do not pay attention to Lyotard's style and its implications for his arguments will miss a productive contribution to thought. Above all, this style is subversive of the status of individual discourses in their pretensions to independence. The capacity of discourses to interrupt one another – and to do so in a convincing manner – is one of the main lessons of *Libidinal Economy*.

The central concept of the book, dissimulation, is an attempt to present that capacity and to allow for a political response to it. True to the ideas it attempts to capture, the work on dissimulation takes place at the cross-over of several discourses and registers. So although it is possible to give a simple abstract definition of the term – *dissimulation is the way in which a system always conceals within itself affects and hence other systems that are inconsistent with it and with each other* – it is restrictive to take that definition as a pure origin or as complete. Similarly, although it is possible to give a relatively straightforward characterisation of Lyotard's libidinal politics – *act so as to release and to hide as much intensity as possible in a given system*, where intensity is defined in terms of the affect that accompanies the lack of common measure or norms between systems – this characterisation, when taken as a self-contradictory maxim, has the potential to draw us far away from what has been achieved in *Libidinal Economy*.

On a hard-nosed epistemological reading of these definitions Lyotard's philosophy does indeed seem to be based on some fantastic and flawed energetics. There is intensity, or energy, hidden in all systems. Our task is to release it. But what is this energy? What evidence do you have for it? Why is it *always* hidden? Why seek to release it rather than bury it deeper in the name of order and harmony? In short, this approach does not allow us to get at Lyotard's arguments and hence to understand or develop a feel for the subtleties of his philosophy. There is no doubt that sometimes he deserves this reading and that may even be desirable as a way of shocking and enticing us into an ultra-revolutionary politics. This is Iain Hamilton

Grant's view in his introduction to *Libidinal Economy* where he stresses the scandalous nature and value of the book: 'This is Lyotard's "evil book", do not expect answers to the questions it generates, nor excuses or rationalisations of its scandals' (xxxi). This view is supported, not only by numerous anti-theoretical statements made throughout *Libidinal Economy* ('So let's struggle against the white terror of truth, by means of and for the red cruelty of singularities', 241) but also in more preparatory essays such as 'March 23'.

This position is also supported in a negative way by Lyotard in a later interview with Van Reijen and Veerman, 'Les lumières, le sublime' in *Les cahiers de philosophie: Jean-François Lyotard, réécrire la modernité*, 63–98, esp. 90–93. The affirmative and 'cruel' philosophy of *Libidinal Economy* is read as 'desperation' and 'nihilism' in order to explain why the book shocked 'its few readers'. I hope to show later in this chapter that this embarrassed revision from the standpoint of the philosophy of the differend is utterly wrong in its statements about the nihilism of the libidinal philosophy. Lyotard explains the desperation through an account of the 'crisis' that he was going through at the time due to the failure of Marxism. I hope to have shown and continue to show that this depiction of a desperate act responding to a psychological crisis is doubly inaccurate.

First, the relation with Marxism is nowhere near as simple as could be understood through the time-span and dynamics implied by the term 'crisis'. *Libidinal Economy* pursues Marxist issues brought up in earlier works, most notably Lyotard's careful readings of Marx in *Dérive à partir de Marx et Freud*. It seeks to resolve them carefully and consistently, albeit in a different style and according to a different set of philosophical terms. Second, irrespective of how Lyotard remembers how he felt around the time of writing *Libidinal Economy*, the main terms that the book introduces and puts into action are not absolute in the sense of 'this terrible moment of nihilism and complete scepticism' ('Les lumières, le sublime': 90). On the contrary, each time such a position looms it is undone with great precision but never with great ease or simplicity: 'It would make us happy to be able to retranscribe, into a libidinal discourse, those intensities which haunt Marx's thought and which, in general, are dissimulated in the brass-tacks solemnity of the discourses of economy and politics' (LE: 104).

It will be shown below that according to the concept of dissimulation Lyotard's attitude to theory could not simply be opposition. It is more of a suspicion of a certain totalising approach to theory and to its libidinal purity. In *Libidinal Economy*, he is concerned with forms of repetition and application. He is also concerned with claims and statements about things, as well as arguments connecting these claims and applications. In short, he is developing and experimenting with a philosophical and political method, but this method must remain fluid and open to change, as opposed to becoming fixed by a permanent theory. Method is then understood as a practical way of responding to a series of problems and challenges associated with the creation of a philosophy and a politics responding to novel events. Beyond pure theory but as method, Lyotard's philosophy does not seek a global representation of a field based on secure philosophical foundations. Instead, a practice emerges and evolves *in vivo* simultaneously in many different fields. We are given tools to experiment with and perhaps to refine or discard in tackling further problems. These are adapted to earlier problems and do not lay claim to a life led independently of them as pure theory. But is this work across boundaries and resistant to abstraction begging the question of the necessity of theory?

Not entirely. One of the main fields to be investigated by Lyotard is theory itself. He is not simply refusing the theoretical 'drive' to interact with a 'given field' in order to change it on the basis of a more 'accurate understanding' of it. It is rather that he refuses to accept the dominant historical assumption that these concepts are set prior to the investigation into their relation to truth. Lyotard sets out to show that theory and representation, as they are commonly defined and relied upon, cannot satisfy the claims that they themselves set. This comes out most clearly in the final chapter of the book, when he reflects on its own status as theory and on the libidinal character of theory and of the concepts highlighted above. Briefly, theory (viewed libidinally) takes pleasure in immobilising and sucking dry its prey through a repetition of the same.

This also explains why theory is co-extensive with a certain function within capitalism – the function that aims to identify a thing in order to reproduce it: 'To think something, is to be able to think it, to produce it and reproduce it. There is no first time, repetition is primary since it is included in the very constitution of the element: concept, commodity. If it is not repeatable, equally exchangeable, it is not an element of the system' (LE: 251). The purity of theory and its concepts is then ruined by the libidinal and economic aspects it conceals within. The Nietzschean aspects of this argument are not made explicit in the relevant passages of *Libidinal Economy*, though Lyotard makes a number of positive references to him elsewhere in the book. But, without direct reference, Lyotard still repeats the libidinal and economic perspective of will to power in Nietzsche's study of the 'Egyptianism' of theoreticians in *Twilight of the Idols*.

This attitude to theory began to gain a more general assent later and with little or no reference to Lyotard's libidinal work. For example, twelve years after the publication of *Libidinal Economy*, the collection *States of Theory* brought together leading writers in the humanities around the question of theory, including Derrida, Jean-Luc Nancy and Lyotard (by now in his sublime/differend phase). Derrida's article is representative of the collection in drawing our attention to the cross-fertilisation of theories, even when they deny it, and to their experimental and fluid nature. He calls them jetties, as in a projection but also a stabilisation. The interaction of theories is seen as partly libidinal and economic, but also national and war-like.

Reflecting on the plurality of theories in the States at the time of writing, Derrida describes the tension between the stabilising and projecting properties of theory. He also describes how this leads to a field of loosely interacting theories and a possible relationship to it:

> [The relationship] would deal with this multiplicity as a law of the field, a clause of non-closure which would not only never allow itself to be ordered and inscribed, . . ., but would also make possible and inevitable synecdochic and metonymic competitions . . . as a means of disseminal alterity or alteration, which would make impossible the pure identity, the pure identification of what it simultaneously makes possible – which would thus delimit and destabilise the state or the establishment to which it gives rise in order for this state or establishment to take place.
>
> ('Some statements and truisms about neologisms, newisms, postisms, parasitisms, and other small seisms': 72)

The use of synecdoche and metonymy in this passage indicates the way in which theories fail in their claim to be totalising: they can be taken as part of a larger theoretical whole, or disassembled and reused for different theoretical purposes. The prescriptive lesson that he suggests is that we should be interested in theoretical monstrous monstrosities 'which never present themselves as such', that is, which escape a straightforward definition or normalisation. Lyotard's work in *Libidinal Economy* is among other things an attempt to show exactly these monsters that 'outdate and make comical all classification and rhythms . . .'.

In line with this view of theory and the multiplicity of perspectives, my reading of *Libidinal Economy* is more a case of searching for emerging patterns and tools for organising them than analysing the text for a dominant, consistent and well-founded theory. Does this mean that the reading is no longer critical? Yes, if critique is to be restricted to the assessment of a philosophy in terms of the validity of a given theory, where validity is in the certainty of a set of foundations and the correctness of the logical arguments that build on this or in the logical correctness of the dialectical moves from a theory to a practice and back again.

Isn't this dialectics exactly what we are talking about when we concentrate on Lyotard's practice? No, the point of practice here and in Lyotard's work is to deny the possibility of making the distinction between theory and practice clear cut, even as a moment in a process that overcomes particular distinctions. However, there is still a sense of critique here, not only in the rather banal sense of studying whether a particular pattern has been followed or reproduced – critique as interest and disinterest, or following on or cutting off – but in the sense of analysing the reasons and impulses we have for that interest or disinterest. Even if in the end these have to be reduced to the contingency of singular desires, the process of reduction is itself critical.

DISSIMULATION IN CONTEXT

In the emergence of the concept of dissimulation in *Libidinal Economy*, the following pattern of topics can be made to stand out.

1. *Poststructuralism and the opposition to meaning as recuperation and exploitation.* Lyotard argues that dissimulation operates as a counter to the structuralist claim that any occurrence, linguistic or otherwise, takes place in a meaningful logical structure. In other words, he seeks to oppose the view that any event is a signifier, the meaning or, more properly, the signified of which can be analysed according to a wider structure of signifiers and signifieds. Everything must then take its place in a pre-given logical system that regulates the way in which meaning emerges. The nature of this counter is not to deny the possibility of analysing an event in this way, but to claim that it is also possible to look at it in another way that is not consistent with a pre-given system (LE: 50). Thus there is not an opposition between sense and the senseless, but a more complex relation of senses, matter and affects (see below). This opposition to meaning does not necessarily have to take place in the context of poststructuralism; for example, in the later Lyotard much of this work takes place through an admittedly rather casual reading of Wittgenstein in 'Wittgenstein, "after"': 'In the *Tractatus*, silence protects the languages of value against the claims of knowledge' (PW: 20).

2. *A politics of flight.* The poststructuralist way is first looked at in terms of a political opposition between: (a) that which is recuperated or put to work within a system (in the case of structuralism this means an event treated as something that contributes new useful meanings to the system; it is a new information to be exploited); and (b) that which escapes the system, or more accurately makes the system leak, setting it in movement towards new possibilities that demand a creative response. Lyotard takes Deleuze and Guattari's term 'line of flight' from *Anti-Oedipus* to characterise this opposition further. There is an opposition between a politics of conquest and a politics of exodus: 'We must first grasp this: signs are not only terms, stages, set in relation and made explicit in a trail of conquest; they *can also* be indissociably, singular and vain intensities in exodus' (50).

3. *An effort to define singularity without having to ground it in an outside.*
There is considerable emphasis on this indissociability in *Libidinal Economy*.
Lyotard goes to great lengths to avoid having to define singularities and
intensities as things which cannot have meaning or cannot be recuperated in
the structuralist sense. He does not want to have to depend on arguments of a
type that posits a beyond logic, meaning, reason or productivity. Arguments
such as 'God is present but incomprehensible' are attacked with greater
vehemence than structuralist theory in the book. I have argued elsewhere that
this is not the case for the philosophy of the differend (Williams 1998: 99–
100). Perhaps this is the great strength of the earlier work; it refuses to fall
back onto a metaphysical religiosity: 'The first thing to avoid, comrades, is
pretending that we are situated elsewhere' (LE: 50). However, despite statements such as this one, Gilles Deleuze and Félix Guattari put forward a
strong argument for the religiosity of Lyotard's libidinal philosophy (Deleuze
1977: 351, analysed in Williams 1998: 129–33).

4. *A distinction between knowing and being affected by a same thing.*
Lyotard insists that there are not different kinds of events or signs. There
are different ways of acting upon them. The recuperation of the sign as
meaning is associated with a cognitive reception, whereas the libidinal
following on (or dance, see below) is associated with a creative movement:
'It speaks to you? It sets us in motion' (LE: 51). So a sign has two sides or
two potentials and this is what he calls the 'duplicity' of signs. A sign can be
taken as something to be inscribed into a pre-existing system as a productive
source of meaning. Or it can be taken as the catalyst for a further creation:
'We do not suppose, to begin with, that the signs, . . . transport messages
that are communicable in principle. We do not start off saying to ourselves:
there is something or someone that *speaks* to us, I must understand them'
(50).

5. *Avant-garde motion defined as dance.* Lyotard is an outstanding writer
on avant-garde art (see, for instance, his book on Jacques Monory,
L'assassinat de l'expérience par la peinture, Monory, where the libidinal
philosophy and the work on the sublime are expanded and made richer
through a sensitive discussion of Monory's paintings). This work on art is
essential to his explanation of what it is to be set in motion in a creative act.
The avant-garde artist breaks with what is known and already understood.
This break is set in motion by affects associated with singularities, that is,
with signs taken on their non-cognitive and non-structural side. Again, it is
important to stress that this artistic motion is not a version of genius or
divine inspiration, in the sense that these are gifts from some great
unknown. The affect is something precise associated with a material thing
(something like: 'this word, this colour tear apart these structures and are
associated with this affect and the emergence of these new structures'). In
the discussion of dissimulation, Lyotard defines this relation in terms of

avant-garde dance and music, as well as Nietzsche's use of dance and the dionysian: 'A dance, then, not composed and notated, but on the contrary, one in which the body's gesture would be, with the music, its timbre, its pitch, intensity and duration, and with the words (dancers are also singers), at each point in a unique relation, becoming at every moment an emotional event . . .' (LE: 51).

6. *Premonition of the sublime event.* Later, by the time of *The Differend*, Lyotard sets great store by the combination of expectation and frustration in the event and the Kantian feeling of the sublime (the *Is it happening?* at TD: 181 and IN: 104–7). In the work on dissimulation, we get two beautiful examples of this combination, but put to a different end, not so much the grand sublime but the intensity of the commonplace; not so much the arrival of the great unknowable, but the concealment of intensity in all signs. The potential for affects, for motion, is also in moments of rest and immobility: 'this waiting must also be loved, just as beautiful, this immobility, just as changing and motive as the fracturing unfolding of the play of the graceful pale hands [in a piece of Nôh theatre]'. In *The Differend* and *Inhuman*, the waiting is associated with an all-too-significant grand scale – Kant on the French revolution, the sublime canvases of Barnett Newman. In the libidinal philosophy, it is in the commonplace, with no need for scale before intensity. In this at least the most anti-egalitarian philosophy is democratic:

> For there is also something we seek in a face in a Montparnasse night, in a voice on the telephone, something about to happen, a wavering or a direct tone of voice, a silence, a fixedness, an eruption; but that doesn't come. And this, far from evoking resentment or disgust, this reserve is loved with the most demanding impatience.
>
> (LE: 52)

As opposed to the political democracy of equality of representation (and the represented equality of subjects), *Libidinal Economy* puts forward a democracy of affect: all events, all structures of meaning are open to the most intense reception.

7. *The type of event is irrelevant; what matters politically is the tension between the two sides of the sign.* The definition of a sign as a site of tension between recuperation as meaning and singular affects associated with the avant-garde dance is essential to the concept of dissimulation. Lyotard defines the sign as a tensor or the place where incommensurable systems come together with a singularity. The affect is itself the sign of that tension.

These definitions imply that any system or structure conceals affects: 'That the structure be something that merely "covers" the affect, in the sense that it acts as a cover: that is its secret and almost its dissimulation' (LE: 52). So every event and every sign is potentially structure and that which escapes structure. This is why there can be no outside the system. It is also why there can be no total system. Instead, there is a covert relation between the two: they hide each other. The metaphors of deception and duplicity are justified in the way in which they express the potential of an ambiguous origin for the acts of uncovering and shrouding that follow it. The sign is only fully exploited – or followed in its intensity – when these acts take it up. These acts are irretrievably linked through that ambiguity: 'Our reception of the sign dissimulates its semiotic reception, which also dissimulates ours . . .' (52). But, although they can never escape each other, the politics of system and of singularity play for different stakes: 'Let us be content to recognize in dissimulation all that we have been seeking, difference within identity, the chance event within the foresight of composition, passion within reason – between each, so absolutely foreign to each other, the strictest unity: dissimulation' (52).

8. *Freudian drives and an argument against polysemy*. It could appear, from what has been said above, that Lyotard's philosophy is consistent with polysemy, a view that the sign is open to a potentially infinite set of different structures and hence different meanings. This would mean that there would be no definitive interpretation, but that nonetheless interpretation in terms of known structures was the only way to respond to the sign. Lyotard turns to Freud's *Beyond the Pleasure Principle* to refute this damaging thesis. He seeks to show that Freud's psychoanalytic theory depends on an undecidable relation between two principles, Eros or the pleasure principle and the death drive. Neither can be treated independently of the other in terms of an understanding of how they function. Any psychic phenomenon is at the same time a function of the death drive and of the pleasure principle. 'In each unique event the functions are undecidable: it is always a question of retaining the possibility that it may not be possible to assign an affect, that is, *simply a sign*, to one pulsional principle and one alone' (54).

According to Lyotard's reading of Freud, it is not so much that a sign can have many different meanings, but that those meanings are only properly interpreted in terms of the sign as interdependent. That dependence must itself be explained in terms of something independent of meaningful structures. This is the sign as a singularity associated with intense affects: 'At the same time a sign which produces meaning through difference and opposition, and a sign producing intensity through force and singularity' (54). 'At the same time' or dissimulation – there is no logical order here, in terms of explanation or analysis or in terms of politics. What matters is to affirm that dissimulation in the sign in order to bring out intensity in structures.

This pattern of topics has been taken from the section on dissimulation in *Libidinal Economy*. Like all the other parts of the book it is very dense and written in the complex style outlined above. The pattern and its components are reproduced in different styles and contexts, and at different lengths throughout the book. It could be said that there is an outline of the arguments and concerns of the book as a whole in this pattern, so long as we add that some key examples and applications have been omitted from the pattern due to the limited treatment of them in the libidinal section. Thus an important discussion of Marx, theory and dialectics is missing, though it is present in the mock-playful concluding lines of the section: 'Is there any need to mention the hilarious perspectives opened up by this idea of dissimulation in matters of theoretical discourse especially in this business (blandly taken on these days under the label of Freudo-Marxism) of the dialectic of theory and practice?' (LE: 54). Also missing are the essential case of colonialism, some examples from art interpretation and the dominant case from the book, the study of capitalism. All of these will be discussed at greater or lesser lengths below and in other chapters.

The effect of the pattern and of its distortion and expansion through the book is to nullify attempts to reduce the book to a single line or style of argument. The points above make important arguments about the nature of signs, the limits of structuralism, why dissimulation is necessary and what politics should respond to it. But these arguments vary greatly in type. There is an *interpretation* of Freud and cases in psychoanalysis. There are *remarks* and *commentaries* on art and the avant-garde. There is an *analysis* of the potential of the sign. There are the beginnings of a *metaphysics* of desire and affects that appears to owe much to Spinoza and Nietzsche. There are many *openings* onto literary and historical texts and passages by a great range of authors, including Lyotard; these openings inject a sense of the breadth and energy of libidinal life (modern and traditional dance; waiting for seduction; Proust; Cage). There is also the *deduction* of a politics of dissimulation with a concomitant rejection of other more absolute forms of politics and philosophy. There is an *application* of all these arguments to a series of cases.

None of these arguments is decisive in the sense that they are either complete, thorough or tested. At best they are interesting conjectures and proposals. At worst they are mere bravado and baiting. In terms of politics and social critique the interest lies mainly in the conjecture about dissimulation; that is, that all systems conceal other systems because they conceal singularities and that Lyotard's libidinal politics consists in hiding and releasing the intensity associated with singularities. At this level, the grounds of the philosophy seem to matter less than its application, what it does and does not allow us to do and say. However, on a different level, it seems important to pursue the style of his philosophy further in terms of how it allows for the creation of patterns of concepts and arguments while avoiding serious contradictions. This pursuit will be taken further through a consideration of how Lyotard avoids a contradictory position on one of his main concerns: the problem of nihilism.

THE PROBLEM OF NIHILISM

> But it is not an ethics, this or another, that is required. Perhaps we need an *ars vitae*, young man, but then one in which we would be the artists and not the propagators, the adventurers and not the theoreticians, the hypothethizers and not the censors.
>
> (LE: 11)

Even if we accept the reading of *Libidinal Economy* as a book of rich hypotheses on how to live free of modern totalisation and religious representations, this does not absolve us of a grave set of contradictions and obscurities threatening to undermine the book. If we work back from the deduction of a politics of dissimulation through Lyotard's analysis of the sign as tensor between structures and singular affects, we encounter what appears to be a serious contradiction. Though he professes to seek a philosophy of affirmation in order to escape nihilism, the book seems to lapse back into the forms of negation that he associates with it. Unlike the nihilism of will that threatens the work on Algeria through the despair at the crushing of modern hopes by the adaptive qualities of capital, this time the risk lies in the formal structure of the arguments of Lyotard's philosophy.

Once again, the link with the Nietzschean argument on the association of negation, critique and nihilism is very strong. However, Lyotard describes a modern set of nihilistic theories and practices, no doubt informed by his work on Algeria and his studies of structuralism and of Freudian negation in *Discours, figure*. He also fails to discuss the more shaded formal account of nihilism that can be extracted from the complex source of Nietzsche's aphorisms. This is done particularly well by Gilles Deleuze in his *Nietzsche and Philosophy*. Deleuze follows Nietzsche to the possibility of a transmutation, a one-way transformation into affirmation, of nihilism through its reactive aspect as the will to negate:

> Thus we can see that the relation between nihilism and transmutation is deeper than was initially suggested. Nihilism expresses the quality of the negative as *ratio cognoscendi* of the will to power; but it cannot be brought to completion without transmuting itself into the opposite quality, into affirmation as *ratio essendi* of this same

will. . . . Destruction becomes active at the moment when, with the alliance between reactive forces and the will to nothingness broken, the will to nothingness is converted and crosses over to the side of affirmation, it is related to the power of affirming which destroys the reactive forces themselves.

(Deleuze 1983: 173)

We come to know will to power through the activity of negating, but it comes into being or has its reason as affirmation. Affirmation is then that which transforms the activity of negation into something positive. It turns away from negation as will to nothingness by affirming the power to negate that will.

This knowledge of will to power is the way for nihilism to transform itself into activity free of negation. It is evidence for the positive role of nihilism in a philosophy of affirmation seeking to avoid a descent into the pure passivity of a 'will to nothingness'. Deleuze's careful set of distinctions is made possible by a taxonomy of active and reactive forces drawn up from Nietzsche's descriptions of different characters (the artist, the noble, and so on). The result of this taxonomy and the study of the relations that hold between its categories is the description of the way out of will to nothingness. According to Deleuze, affirmation is doubly related to negation as the negation of nihilism and the destruction of values: 'Destruction as the active destruction of the man who wants to perish and to be overcome announces the creator'; 'Destruction as the active destruction of all known values is the trail of the creator' (Deleuze 1983: 177).

Lyotard's approach is very different. He enacts nihilism by creating new glimpses of nihilistic characters (the semiotician, for example) and tossing them into contemporary theories and situations. The latter owes more to Nietzsche's style of thought and to the idea that affirmation lies in that style. The former owes more to Nietzsche's capacity to draw subtle conceptual distinctions while still maintaining a well-structured, if concealed, argument. Does this distinction go further? Does *Libidinal Economy* satisfy Deleuze's requirements for an affirmative philosophy, in treating values and nihilist thought as something to be destroyed in order to make way for affirmation? Or is it simply a book of resentful contradictions, re-erecting a logic of negation in a philosophy of pure desire? On the one hand, *Libidinal Economy* could be *Nietzsche and Philosophy* brought to life and drawn away from the dangers of a status as definitive theory. On the other hand, it could be a pathetic gesture caught in the naïve ignorance of Nietzsche's and Deleuze's insights.

The focus of Lyotard's concern with nihilism is in the divide opened up between the signifier and what it signifies, or between the theoretical or religious representation and what is represented. He calls this divide the 'great zero'. This zero or divide holds the matter of the sign away from its sense. It does so with an implicit direction and value. We must move from the matter to the sense, from sensation or affect to meaning and understanding. This movement is always incomplete, whether according to the model of religiosity, where sense is always beyond our finite understanding, or according to the modern model of science, where sense is always a work in progress and part of an infinite regress of meanings with no final origin:

> Not only is the material commuted into a sign-term, but also the 'thing' which the sign replaces is itself another sign, there is nothing but signs. First consequence: the relation is therefore an infinite postponement, and thus sets up recurrence as a fundamental trait of the system, the reiteration of the *postponement of the signifier* guaranteeing that one will always need to work to determine the terms to which, in a given *corpus*, the term under examination can and must lead. The other consequence is that with the sign begins the *search*.
>
> (LE: 44–5)

The models of religion and structuralist science share a necessary devaluation of matter and affect in favour of understanding. But in sharing this they also share a necessary nihilism, since in denying themselves the affect and the desire for the affect and in setting off on a voyage of discovery that cannot end, they set themselves an impossible task. Lyotard's choice of the term 'great zero' is not only an allusion to the absolute and ultimately nihilistic nature of the divide but also to its role in reducing all things to the measure of meaning and understanding.

The turn away from the affect is doubly damaging because, according to Lyotard's work on Freudian negation in *Discours, figure* (116–34; discussed in Williams 1998: 50–54) and *Libidinal Economy*, the turn carries the desire for the affect with it. There is a remnant of the intensity of the affect that accompanies a material event – a caress, a smell – in the desire for God or for absolute knowledge (LE: 47). However, this remnant takes on a vitiated form. Instead of a desire for the movement of the affect, now rendered impossible and secondary, there is a desire for a conceptual completeness, that is, to possess full understanding. This desire for conceptual identity should be, but cannot be fulfilled in the identity of a knowing subject: 'One further consequence for the informational constitution of the sign: there is someone for whom the message replaces the thing signified, there is a subject (two subjects), that is to say an instance to which all the predicates, all the postponements of meaning, all the events experienced and toured, are related' (LE: 48).

The stress on two subjects indicates the split between the subject to whom the communication is supposed to be addressed and the subject deciphering the meaning. There is therefore a split into a receptive and an active part. But for Lyotard this division is the reproduction of the great zero within the subject. Every material experience becomes a sign for interpretation in a dialectic of 'receptive/active, sensible/intelligent, donee/donor' destined to suppress the intensity of affects in understanding. This dialectic is religious, that is, nihilist because the will to interpret is destined to failure: '[Semiotics] is a religious science because it is haunted by the hypothesis that someone speaks to us in these givens and, at the same time, that its language, its competence, or in any case its performative capacity transcends us' (LE: 49). But what is the critique of semiotics, if not a rather old and familiar step towards nihilism in the loss of belief in the values of religion, science and the subject?

The answer lies in Lyotard's claim that dissimulation is universal. Despite his attacks on the nihilism of religion, structuralism, critique and theory, his philosophy is not consistent with the aim to have done with nihilism, or indeed with theory and critique, once and for all. On the contrary, if there can be a libidinal philosophy of intensity and affects it will only take place within structures, within negation and within theory. So it is rather an opposition to absolute exclusions, wherever they come from, that characterises his work: '. . . it is in no way a matter of determining a new domain, another field, a beyond representation which would be immune to the effects of theatricality, not at all, we are well aware that you are just waiting for us to do this, to be so "stupid" . . .' (LE: 50).

So the way to live with nihilism is not to avoid structures and systems of negation, but to draw out the intensities, the affects and desires that they hide, in order to allow for further creations, further opportunities for their concealment and release. In the case of the nihilism of the search for meaning, the key lies in the affects associated with the desire to search for and hoard meanings. This has a negative side, in the sense of the desire to capitalise on a new sensation, a new discovery. But it has a positive side in the risk of destabilisation and transformation in the encounter of the strange materials that we are driven towards. This encounter does not depend upon a pure materiality, the doomed dream of an experience of something that cannot be a sign. Rather, it depends upon Lyotard's hypothesis that signs are 'duplicitous', that is, that they are open to a reading that stores them as meaning and capital, but that they are also open to a reception that defeats capitalisation through the release of intensity:

> *Like those of capital*, these signs are duplicitous, and there is no question of declaring *urbi et orbi* that with their appearance semiotics and political economics are ruined, and desire emancipated from the stocks of the system of values. Their intensity is new, in the manner in which they are inscribed into established regions,

by the distances which they force back and evoke. Rather than greeting a new dawn, we should honour the new dissimulation in them.

(LE: 94)

Lyotard compresses Deleuze's treatment of nihilism as constitutive of affirmation into the concepts of dissimulation and duplicity. The sign can be received in a nihilistic or in an affirmative way, but neither of these can exclude the other. They are interdependent because the intense sign has to be 'inscribed into established regions'.

But this seems to be the worst form of equivocation. If affirmation and negation are so closely related, if the sign is duplicitous in this ineluctable manner, then does that not plunge us back into a position where no precise course of action is possible, where an affirmative creative act cannot be distinguished from a negative one? Is not this the sure-fire way to a final 'will to nothingness'?

Deleuze answers this objection by drawing a distinction between opposition and differing, one that he develops with great care after *Nietzsche and Philosophy*, most notably in *Difference and Repetition*. Negation is opposition, affirmation is differing: 'Negation is *opposed* to affirmation but affirmation *differs* from negation' (188). As opposed to the final 'this is not this' of negation, affirmation says 'this becoming this becoming this . . .'. Where the former defines a fixed being through opposition, the latter adopts a contingent differing from one differing to others: 'Affirmation is posited for the first time as multiplicity, becoming and chance. For multiplicity is the difference of one thing from another, becoming is difference from self and chance is difference "between all" or distributive difference' (189).

So when we say correctly that negation is as much a quality of will to power as affirmation, we are not committed to saying that will to power is the same in negation and affirmation: 'If we understand affirmation and negation as qualities of the will to power we see that they do not have a univocal relation' (188). Negation posits being and necessity according to absolute differences. Affirmation is becoming, multiplicity and chance and their affirmation (Deleuze calls this redoubled affirmation).

To affirm is not simply to not negate; it is to redouble differing as becoming, multiplicity and chance. There is a transmutation of nihilism as destruction and negation in affirmation, but it is destruction by chance, not by necessity; it is negation by differing and multiplicity, not by opposition. Yet can we read Lyotard's use of critique, his attacks on negation in this way? Does his definition of dissimulation draw up something akin to, or as effective as, Deleuze's redoubled affirmation? In short, how does Lyotard distinguish a libidinal politics from a politics of systematisation without falling into the pathos of simply negating systems in favour of something that is supposed to be free of negation?

53

HEIDEGGER AND METAPHYSICS

This pathos of the return of nihilism is described with great force and beauty by Heidegger, in particular in his books and essays on Nietzsche (*Nietzsche*; 'The Word of Nietzsche: "God is Dead"' in Heidegger 1977). His argument is of use here because it adds a different way of thinking about nihilism as well as providing a balance to Deleuze's interpretation of Nietzsche as a transvaluation of nihilism. Heidegger argues that Nietzsche's philosophy is still nihilistic, even when it makes the essential link between metaphysics and nihilism. The simple version of this argument is that Nietzsche's philosophy remains metaphysical in its logic of negation and therefore nihilistic:

> Nevertheless, as a mere countermovement it necessarily remains, as does everything "anti," held fast in the essence of that over against which it moves. Nietzsche's countermovement against metaphysics is, as a mere turning upside down of metaphysics, an inextricable entanglement in metaphysics, in such a way, indeed, that metaphysics is cut off from its essence and, as metaphysics, is never able to think its own essence.

> (Heidegger 1977: 61)

Heidegger's general line of argument goes from a Nietzschean definition of metaphysics as dependent on a positing of the 'suprasensory' or transcendent world as true and real, as opposed to the devalued physical world that depends upon it for any sense and value. It then follows a path similar to Lyotard's argument on the nihilistic consequences of the continual postponement that follows a search for value in a suprasensory, unattainable, world. But Heidegger adds an interpretation of Nietzsche's will to power as value-setting that shows it to be a metaphysical concept dependent on the 'mere turning upside down' of earlier metaphysical values.

According to Heidegger, will to power is a negation of the suprasensory that remains metaphysical because it defines a new foundation and value that it imposes on Being. Man and the setting of values associated with establishing man as will to power are this foundation and these values. He interprets will to power as the preserving and increasing of human will as value: 'The struggle for dominion over the earth is in its historical essence already the result of the fact that whatever is as such is appearing in the mode of the will to power without yet being recognized or without being understood at all as that will' (101). His commentary on Nietzsche's word 'God is dead' allows him to put all this in the context of a replacement of God, as suprasensible value, by man as the will to the power to set values. The contemporary thoroughgoing technological world may appear to retain

God, may appear to look to suprasensible values, but as such it is already the world of Nietzsche's will to power.

So it is not simply that metaphysics turns away from this world towards an unattainable suprasensory world that makes it nihilistic. It is that its structure of foundation and value-setting 'forgets' or 'covers up' existence as something which is neither a suprasensible idea nor willing, but that appears in both. Thinking is nihilistic when it turns to these ideas and when it looks to its own power to create values. Indeed, 'existence' is usually defined in these terms and that which is forgotten is best allowed to appear as 'being': that which appears indirectly when thinking is not satisfied with a final idea or set of values. The thought of being or, more properly, Being, and its forgetting is one of the most demanding, but also one of the most important aspects of Heidegger's thought. It is not satisfactory to define these terms negatively except in the name of limited space and time and with the proviso that these definitions should be added to by further reading. For example, Miguel de Beistegui's *Heidegger and the Political* contains an enlightening discussion of these issues in the context of a wider study of Heidegger and nihilism (63–86). The most important aspect of Heidegger's writing on being and nihilism for this study of Lyotard's nihilism is the refusal to pin down being to specific human activities (including definition): 'Yet even thinking, understood in the most originary sense, or for that matter, poetizing, to say nothing of all other human "activities," cannot of themselves bring about [the turn toward the truth of being]' (de Beistegui 1998: 83). This remains only a 'possibility'.

Nietzsche's philosophy of will to power is interpreted by Heidegger as having exactly the structure of the metaphysical forgetting of being through the emergence of man as foundation for value-positing: 'The value-thinking of the metaphysics of the will to power is murderous in a most extreme sense, because it absolutely does not let Being itself take its rise, i.e., come into the vitality of its essence. Thinking in terms of values precludes in advance that Being itself will attain to a coming to presence in its truth' (108). Metaphysics is then the violence of an imposition of values on the basis of a structure that itself imposes a value. In Heidegger's interpretation of Nietzsche, in parallel to his interpretation of our contemporary values and actions, man has taken the place of God or the suprasensible. Man's values and the value of man are, for instance, modern technology and its focus on the world transformed for man and according to man's values ('the truth of what is as such').

But Being is not in this historical process and its principles. Nihilism is then claimed to have eclipsed Being in favour of the product of this process, the 'whatever is as such' or, to follow Derrida, 'presence':

> The essence of nihilism lies in history; accordingly, in the appearing
> of whatever is as such, in its entirety, Nothing is befalling Being

55

itself and its truth, and indeed in such a way that the truth of what is as such passes for Being, because the truth of Being remains wanting. In the age of that completion and consummation of nihilism which is beginning, Nietzsche indeed experienced some characteristics of nihilism, and at the same time he explained them nihilistically, thus completely eclipsing their essence.

(109)

For Heidegger, nihilism is not Lyotard's 'great zero', the divide that opens up between intensity and a constantly deferred sense; it is any thought of the 'as such', something that is assumed to be present to us in its entirety.

But is this view inconsistent with the spirit of Lyotard's libidinal philosophy – less in its negation of the suprasensible, for that is rightly to be called nihilism in the Heideggerian sense, but in the way that it seeks to avoid and go beyond this negation without falling back into metaphysics? Heidegger's interpretation of Nietzsche does not allow for the possibility that will to power is an attempt to go beyond this negation. But it is possible to interpret will to power in this way and thereby to avoid its reduction to human will and hence to a metaphysical foundation. Deleuze's definition of affirmation given above is exactly one such interpretation. Heidegger defines will to power as that out of which metaphysics returns to the subject ('subjectness'), to certainty, to consciousness of truth in itself, to 'self-willing' (Heidegger 1977: 101).

This is a very strict interpretation of will when compared to Deleuze's association of will to power as affirmation with 'becoming, multiplicity and chance' (*Nietzsche and Philosophy*: 190). Heidegger attributes the following to the 'necessary' relation of will to power and consciousness:

Making conscious is a necessary instrument of the willing that wills from out of the will to power. It happens, in respect to objectification, in the form of planning. It happens, in the sphere of the uprising of man into self-willing, through the ceaseless dissection of the historical situation. Thought metaphysically, the 'situation' is constantly the stage for the action of the subject. Every analysis of the situation is grounded, whether it knows it or not, in the metaphysics of subjectness.

(Heidegger 1977: 102)

But will to power, as viewed by Deleuze, is the defeat of consciousness as a capacity to gather and identify; it is the affirmation of multiplicity and not the identity of the object or the self. Will to power is not planning; it is chance. It is not the action of the subject, but a passive openness through the redoubling of that which undoes the identity of the subject. Does Lyotard allow for any clarification of this difference of interpretations?

More precisely, does Lyotard allow for a more practical example of this apparent contradiction 'passive will to power'?

THE POLITICAL AS ACTIVE PASSIVITY

Lyotard risks an answer to these questions in the last section of *Libidinal Economy*. These explicit answers, however, are the guiding principles that give coherence to the book as a whole, as much in terms of style as in terms of arguments. They explain how the libidinal philosophy can escape the nihilism that it reacts to and builds up so strongly. Part of the answer acknowledges some link to Heidegger's response to the problem, though at best the comments have to be seen as jocular with a serious undercurrent. At worst they betray a visceral animosity and mistrust for the thinker and his much discussed involvement with National Socialism (see de Bestegui, *Heidegger and the Political*, for a considered response to this involvement; see Farias, *Heidegger and Nazism*, for the most influential source implicating Heidegger in Nazism; see Lacoue-Labarthe, *La fiction du politique*, for a paradigm of the difficulties this implication causes for deconstruction).

Lyotard covers this involvement in greatest depth some time after *Libidinal Economy* in his *Heidegger et 'les juifs'*. He argues that Heidegger is incapable of thinking the Other and that therein lies the real fault of his politics. The later Lyotard expresses this thought of the Other in terms of 'the Law' we are hostage to: we have to take on the impossible task of testifying to the Other. Heidegger's thinking 'stays established in thinking Being, in the "Western" prejudice that the Other is being, it has nothing to say about a thinking the Other as Law' (Lyotard 1988b: 145). Lyotard's determined criticism of Heidegger and of other thinkers who follow him, albeit uneasily, into 'onto-deconstruction' can be explained by his ever-present concern with how to think after Auschwitz.

From his earliest essay, 'Born in 1925', through 'Discussions, or phrasing "after Auschwitz"' up to the *Heidegger et 'les juifs'* book and essay of the same name, Lyotard has struggled with the destruction of any possible community, or 'we', that could think Auschwitz: 'There would not even be a spirit, a spirit of the people or a spirit of the world, which are "*wes*", to repossess the name "Auschwitz", to think it and to think itself inside it' (Lyotard 1989b: 376). The only possible just response is then one that testifies to a paradoxical Law that says that there is the Other that cannot be thought. For Lyotard, Heidegger still allows for a community around the question of the forgetting of Being and this means that he has to forget that after Auschwitz such a community is not possible: 'I think that Heidegger's silence [on the Holocaust] is due to another *Stellung* [enframing], another closure, and another forgetting: the exclusion of what I have called the event of the covenant, the forgetting of a silent law that takes the soul hostage and forces it to bear witness to the violent obligation it has undergone' (Lyotard 1988b: 147). For Lyotard, Heidegger's fault lies in his failure to attempt to testify to that which cannot be said about specific events. We are obliged to testify to injustice, despite the necessary inadequacy of our testimony.

There is a faint connection between these remarks and the comments in *Libidinal Economy* since there the reference to Heidegger takes place around the problem of the impossibility of poetry as a way of thinking Being:

> If there is a profound failure, an impossibility, of poetry today, it is not because we live in troubled times and that Being has withdrawn from us. This discourse of profound reasons bores the hell out of us. Nothing has withdrawn, we have not 'forgotten' anything; the ancient Greeks, Heraclitus, the in-between of faith and knowledge, are no more originary than Janis Joplin.
>
> (LE: 257)

Yet, for the early Lyotard, the impossibility is also not due to the paradoxical law that appears in his work around the time of *Just Gaming*. It is due to dissimulation, that is, that any discourse must remain in the grip of systematisation and what Heidegger calls metaphysics: 'The failure of poetry is simply the impossibility of anti-theory . . .' (LE: 257).

It should be noted that although Lyotard is right in ascribing the forgotten in Heidegger to Greece, Heraclitus and the in-between, this cannot easily be extended into the claim that they are originary in his work; in fact, Heidegger is very careful to avoid making such a claim. It is fair to say, though, that when Heidegger attempts to think the forgetting of Being he does so in a nostalgic and homely fashion (a lost Germany and a lost Greece). It is tempting to follow Lyotard into seeing this as a necessary turn away from Janis Joplin, but at least here the lack of full argument restricts us to appreciating his irony – and good taste?

In response to the failure of a self-contradictory and nihilistic anti-theory, Lyotard sketches the following pattern of remarks that point the way towards a strategy for releasing intense affects, multiplicity and chance within theory.

1. *Seek powerlessness* through a blurring of the borders between what is discussed and the theory that discusses it. This blurring can be achieved by allowing chance to govern those borders. Lyotard often juxtaposes critical remarks, theory and vivid description in a chaotic and open-ended manner. This tactic undoes representation by forcing the reader to reconstitute the relation between them: 'it would let the plugging in of its uncertain border

with that of its client body take place in an aleatory fashion, without bothering to control it' (LE: 255).

2. *Multiply principles of enunciation.* Lyotard not only renders uncertain the distinction between theory, critique and what is theorised. He multiplies the genres used within each. This is done in a radical way such that no one genre dominates or serves as an organising principle for others. Again, this does not make a reductive reading impossible, but it multiplies the points at which a response may take an unexpected and revitalising direction: 'These would be only diverse pieces, each piece of variable format and belonging to its own time with which it begins and ends – pieces which might or might not find their place here and there . . .' (LE: 256).

3. *Accept that failure is necessary.* But more than that, *invite failure into discourse.* Dissimulation implies that any discourse is open to system-atisation or fragmentation into affects and new systems. Once this necessity has been accepted, the paranoia involved in writing for a pure system or for a pure anti-theory is deposed from its prime role in writing and acting:

> Fucking ought not to be guaranteed, in either sense, neither as proof of love nor as the security of indifferent exchangeability; love, that is to say intensity, should slip in in an aleatory fashion, and conversely intensities may withdraw from the skins of bodies (you didn't come?), and pass onto the skins of words, sounds, colours, culinary tastes, animal smells, and perfumes, this is the dissimulation we will not escape, this is the anxiety and this is what we must *will*.
>
> (LE: 256)

In addition to these three principles of passive affirmation, there are also principles of active negation. These cannot properly be taken for principles without the three passively affirmative ones since if they are taken as final they return us to negation. We must pay attention to what is occurring to us, to the power of passivity, by observing the passing of negation.

4. *Do not will as a free subject selecting outcomes or affirm what occurs as necessary.* It is nihilistic to combine the free selection of the outcome I desire and belief in dissimulation, since neither that 'I' nor that outcome have a secure identity. They are always open to being shattered into multiple affects and systems. To will with no nihilistic illusions is to will no outcomes by allowing the chance of many. It is to will no subject by staying open to a multiplicity of affects and hence systems: 'sufficiently refining ourselves, . . . becoming sufficiently anonymous conducting bodies, not in order to stop the effects, but to conduct them into new metamorphoses . . .' (LE 258).

What we have is a given to be worked with and opened up, hence affirmed through blurring, multiplication and failure.

5. The same is true for the influence of the subject. In affirming what occurs, *we seek anonymity by abandoning analysis.* Allow for the possibility that the ego, the self, property, not disappear, but become disinvested in libidinal energy. Anonymity is a tactic for undoing the organising power of the self and the subject, in terms of intensities and wider systems. Do not analyse events (through the self): '[The Freudian analytic relation] is also the search for causes, responsibilities, the search for identity, the localization of desire, becoming conscious, masculinization, power knowledge: that is, analysis' (LE: 259).

6. *Do not believe that you can choose which affects to conduct.* The essential passivity of a selecting will is as much valid for the sensations associated with affects to be conducted as to the possibility of their conduction. So it is not a matter of remaining open solely for pleasure and not for pain. Neither is it a matter of associating pain solely with systems. It is therefore not a matter of desiring this or that, but a matter of letting desire flow (possibly). An affect dissimulates pain as much as it dissimulates pleasure – the pleasure of the transport to a new singular state, but also the pain of leaving a system, including the self. For all that he owes to Spinoza, Lyotard refuses to extend the parallel between his good conduction of intensities and Spinoza's power and conatus. Pain and sadness are not excluded from an increase in power: 'to fix the meaning of the passage, of suffering or of joy, is the business of consciousnesses and their directors' (LE: 42). This is the main reason why a Spinozist community and republicanism cannot emerge from libidinal economy: there is no direction, there are no common notions that rationally limit our passions and that thereby help to form a rational community.

These points answer Heidegger's version of nihilism and its study of presence and the 'as such'. Lyotard's strategy for the good conduction of intensities does not depend on identifying anything or on the attempt to make something our property. It does not allow for settling for any given theory or system, because of his account of dissimulation. On the contrary, it depends on acts that may unsettle them. It does so by inviting that which underlies the subject to disassemble it, but with no dependence on the Heideggerian interpretation of Nietzschean will to power and its capacity to will values. Lyotard is much closer to Heidegger and to a thought where 'the constellation of Being utters itself to us' than he cares to admit. He returns to Heidegger's writing on the event (*Ereignis*) in his work on the event in *The Differend* (74–5). With great difficulty, Lyotard separates his thought on the event from Heidegger's questions on the lightning flash of Being

('Will we see the lightning flash of Being in the essence of technology?', 'The Turning': 49). As in his work on Heidegger and the Law, the crux of the argument turns on the issue of whether he sets parameters for the event by describing the flash as for Man and whereby man fulfils his destiny (75). But the event for the later Lyotard is rather the feeling that it could be for no one and fulfil no destiny: 'That linkage [on from the event] must be made, but there won't be anything on which to link' (TD: 75).

The suspicion is, then, that Heidegger still allows for the possibility that 'we' may become aware of Being: 'Will we dwell as those at home in nearness, so that we will belong primarily within the fourfold of sky, earth, mortals and divinities?' But, for Lyotard's sublime event this question concedes too much to the possibility and specificity of a mythical people and a life at the expense of others, or more properly, the Other. This is true in a different way for Lyotard's account in *Libidinal Economy*. A libidinal politics seeks to conduct intensity through all things. It does so passively, not only in terms of expected outcomes, but also in terms of the multiplicity of systems and affects through which intensity is conducted. In the next chapter, this active passivity will be studied in the context of capitalism and the critical question of whether passivity amounts to political collaboration and lack of power.

4

LIBIDINAL ECONOMY AND CAPITAL

PROBLEMS OF A PASSIVE POLITICS

> But Zeami's semiotics seem to be passed through, sometimes
> thwarted, by a quite different impulse, a pulsionnal drive, a
> search for intensity, a desire for power . . . Signs are then no
> longer taken in their representative dimension. They do not
> even represent Nothingness. They do not represent, they allow
> 'actions'. They function like transformers that consume
> natural and social energies in order to produce affects of
> great intensity.
>
> (DP: 92)

Active passivity, in the sense of a strategy designed to let things affect one
unconsciously, is a logical conclusion of the drift away from the subject and
from systematic control. In the libidinal Lyotard, passivity is an essential
part of politics and morality, understood as a way of living. This conclusion
can also be found in Gilles Deleuze, in the *Logic of Sense* in particular, but
on closer inspection throughout his work, and in Michel Foucault in *The
History of Sexuality*, but also in his work viewed as a whole if we follow
Deleuze's reading in his *Foucault*. In each case a new energy or intensity is
sought to replace the source of political hope and effort associated with the
values of the human subject and our belief in its power to realise them. The
capacity to act upon things reliably, as if external structures mirror the
internal states of the subject (its desires, dreams and ideals), has become
suspect with these thinkers. Can they replace it with an alternative political
strategy?

This question explains why nihilism is of such concern to Lyotard, as it is
for Deleuze and for Foucault, if not explicitly at least implicitly in the
development of his work and in the eyes of his critics. In the loss of the
power of the subject to will things, it appears that the world is reduced
to nothing. But this also explains why the three thinkers seek to redefine

power as the openness to intense sources of change and the capacity to conduct intensity. If we accept that in both approaches the interest in power lies in the opposition between decay, defined as lack of energy, and creation, defined as a surplus of transformative energy, then the difference lies in the source of that power and the way in which it is brought to bear on life.

In the case of the philosophy of the subject, power finds a privileged source in the will of the subject. It is the well-being of that subject and its extension into the world that ensures a growth in power. In the opposite case, power is the capacity to conduct without the representational capacities of the subject. Something flows through without being represented and then willed. An increase in power becomes a difficult trade-off between an increase in the intensity of flows, an increase in their connectedness and an increase in their number. Of course, this increase cannot be willed directly.

So any opposition between the positions sketched above does not lie with the will as such. It lies with the privileging of the will, defined in terms of representation, desire and organic needs, as the source of increases in power. Lyotard, Deleuze and Foucault do not deny that there are such things as decisions and that these decisions can be defined in part in terms of something that makes the decision. What they do deny is that this decision is wholly explicable in terms of free will, that this something is in full possession of any part of itself when it makes a decision, or that the proper goal of the decision in terms of power is directly to take possession of something that has been represented. So they do not fall into a performative contradiction of the form 'I deny that there is a subject'. It is rather that they say 'There is something more than the subject in all of its actions. That something cannot be approached through representation and consciousness. So it cannot be willed. Yet power lies in that something.' Thus the philosophy of passivity is not straightforwardly nihilistic, since it affirms power. Neither is it straightforwardly self-contradictory, since it does not deny the possibility of actions that have been decided upon; it is just that those actions only approach power obliquely.

But how is this power known, if not by representation? How are oblique actions to be guaranteed, and hence guaranteed against nihilism, if not by the direct representation of goals or values? These questions challenge Lyotard to explain why his philosophy is not the simple paradox of an anti-theory and why it is not reduced to a position where no decision is possible in the face of an indistinct chaos. The first question has been answered in the previous chapter through the idea of dissimulation. The belief that theory and representation are governed by a law of either/or (either theory, representation, consciousness or pure sensation, pure intensity) is a false one; instead it is a question of both/and (theory dissimulates intensity and intensity dissimulates theory). The second question is more difficult. What exactly is a passive activity? How does it avoid nihilism in practice? More precisely, why does it not fall prey to the return of nihilistic forces? Is it possible to put forward a politics that can resist capitalism without falling back into resistance as pure negation?

ART AND THE POLITICAL AS ACTIVE PASSIVITY

In the collection of essays that prepares the way for *Libidinal Economy*, *Des Dispositifs pulsionnels*, Lyotard tries to answer these questions in the context of modern art. He defines modern art as an active passivity that breaks with the tradition of representation. But more than this, he begins to write about art as governed by dissimulation, as defined in *Libidinal Economy*: all art is both representative and intense. The question is how to create in response to art forms and materials so as to exploit that dissimulation to the full: 'so all those calculations, the painter's measurements, the formations of tense rules and habits, the actor's training, are not there to show their futility, as Western nihilists believe. They are there to make possible what Zeami calls the *wonderful flower* and its *evanescence*, that is, the effect of the most strange emotion in an instant that cannot be located' (DP: 223). How can we maximise intensity in structures that are also open to a response in terms of further structures and representations?

The artistic approach to the possibility of power through passivity allows Lyotard to make much clearer his libidinal philosophy on the relation between structures (the dominant methods or dispositions in the history of art), representation and the intensity of affects. However, the essays in *Des Dispositifs pulsionnels* also hinder the emergence of a libidinal philosophy in two significant ways that are overcome in *Libidinal Economy*. First, like this work, they are still essays *about* a topic; that is, they remain theoretical in a way that is overcome by the dissimulating style of the later book.

An awareness of this necessary move comes out in the essay 'Adorno come diavolo', where Lyotard experiments with a rather crude passivity in his own discourse by adopting a method loosely related to Burroughs and Gysin's (Burroughs and Odier 1970) cut-up and fold-in method and to David Bowie's passive construction of lyrics: 'I determined six ideas (dialectical, critical, indifference, position, theology and expression, affirmation) within which I distributed all my thoughts in the form of items. A first draw assigned each idea to the face of a die. A second draw (with the die) allowed the diachronic order of appearance of the ideas to be established' (DP: 116). Further draws are then used to redistribute thoughts within the series. The essay then takes on a chance-driven form where something outside conscious intention undermines an established order and turns a critical work about Adorno into a much looser and more suggestive opportunity for ideas. This allows for greater intensity to pass through the work by loosening the grip of theory and structure: 'The artist no longer composes, he lets desire run through his disposition. That is affirmation' ('Adorno come diavolo': 116). But this method is disappointing when compared to the much more thorough and minute attention to style in *Libidinal Economy*. Lyotard realised that a crude mechanics of chance, applied after thoughts had been selected and expressed, came nowhere near intensity when compared to the search for passivity in the flow of writing and topics as they are being written.

There are many resonances with other thinkers in the late sixties and early seventies in this experimentation with the passive undermining of traditional structures. The passage from 'Adorno come diavolo' to *Libidinal Economy* is quite similar to the move Philippe Sollers made from his much-admired early works (*Nombres, Drame, Lois, H*) to the later stream-of-consciousness work *Paradis*. The early works depend on a conscious use of modernist techniques to bring chance and uncertainty into their construction and reception (see Roland Barthes's *Sollers Ecrivain*). But the later work achieves a higher degree of openness and uncertainty by adding an unconscious aleatory factor to the occurrence of words and ideas in addition to the technique of the absence of punctuation marks. Sollers, like Lyotard in *Libidinal Economy*, allows unconscious impulses to provide a disorganised flow of competing discourses, styles and topics. These techniques are new in Lyotard's and Sollers's works, but they are not new as such. Sollers spends much time acknowledging his debt to Joyce (see his discussion with Jean-Louis Houdebine, 'La Trinité de Joyce' in *Tel Quel* 1980). Similarly, Lyotard is greatly influenced by Gertrude Stein, not only in terms of style but also in terms of philosophy of language (*The Differend*: 67–8).

Lyotard describes the passive creative process that works through *Libidinal Economy* thus:

> we are [this book's] effect, pushed aside, and to do this, there are a
> few moments, a dozen moments . . . an idea on fire, an image, the
> smell of a tear gas grenade or an intolerable denial of justice, a face,
> a book, a tensor sign we had to act on, conducting it and letting it
> course through a few quick pages, rapidly arranging words into
> sentences and paragraphs, so that this heat and its chill, this force,
> may pass through.
>
> (LE: 260)

What distinguishes the work from others is his attempt to bring this way of thinking and writing into philosophy. It is another reason why *Libidinal Economy* is an important book. It is rare not only in professing passivity as the way out of the death of the subject, but also in taking the risk of acting it out as philosophy:

> Stop confusing servitude with dependence. We would like a book of complete dependence: these pieces of the ephemeral patchwork would be composed and added to the body, the fingertips, all over the sheets; and these formations would, for a moment, make us dependent upon them.
>
> (LE: 261)

I shall return to this important passage below.

However, the extension of passivity into philosophy and politics is the second reason why the essays in *Des Dispositifs pulsionnels* are a hindrance as much as a help. This extension cannot take place easily so long as art is seen as the key to passivity. Lyotard learnt much from Cézanne, Cage, Zeami, Delaunay and Monory about the ways in which we can allow intensities to flow through works as well as undermine and renew structures. But his essays on them run the risk of limiting libidinal economy to an aesthetics understood solely as art and to the marginal position of the avant-garde artist. This would be a return to the positing of an outside of society, a 'good' region that somehow escapes the negative structures of representation and tradition – if only for as long as it was avant-garde and not recuperated.

At times, Lyotard tends towards this neo-romanticism; for example, whenever he puts hippy movements forward as the example of great intensity: 'Here are today's "supermen" and "masters": the fringe, experimental painters, pop, hippies and yippies, parasites, madmen, internees? There is more intensity and less intention in one hour of their life than in a thousand words by a professional philosopher' ('Notes sur le retour et le capital' at DP: 305). Indeed, the nostalgic, romantic reaction to the dominance of capitalism is a challenge to him since it appears to understand the libidinal potential of capital. But romanticism chooses to use this potential to look back rather than forward. Lyotard investigates this quite beautifully through a study of Baudelaire and 'dandyism' in *L'assassinat de l'expérience par la peinture, Monory* (56–108, esp. 102). However, in the previous chapter, I showed how dissimulation operated in all discourses and how Lyotard uses this to attack any philosophy promising a privileged region or practice. The importance of his work on art, then, is not as aesthetics but as a prolegomenon to a more general libidinal economy and politics of active passivity. So in the following sections his essays on modern art will be read against a fringe politics and in the light of the libidinal economic revaluation of philosophy.

PAINTING AND DESIRE

Lyotard's work on art, structuralism and Freud begins with his French major doctoral dissertation (*Doctorat d'État*) published as *Discours, figure*

(Lyotard passed the French *agrégation* in 1958 and became a Docteur ès Lettres in 1971). The advocacy of figure and affect against structure and sense, and the critical stance with respect to structuralism and phenomenology in that book are then worked into the more political and libidinal essays in *Des Dispositifs pulsionnels*. It is worth noting that the critical reading of phenomenology dates back to even before the essays on Algeria – see *La Phénoménologie* (1954) – though at that stage, the critique was couched in terms of the problems raised for phenomenology in a materialist reading of history.

In order to cover Lyotard's argument in depth, I will follow the argument put forward in one of the essays, 'La peinture comme dispositif libidinal', making cross-references to other works as necessary. The essay is divided into a set of theoretical remarks, followed by a chronological series of analyses of particular works. This divide and order is contradicted by the main findings of the essay. This is why it is best taken as a springboard for the work in *Libidinal Economy* rather than as a free-standing philosophy of painting. It would be better to think of the essays as tending towards art with philosophy (and also not towards philosophy as art) Lyotard does not only investigate the relation of philosophy to painting. The essay 'La dent, la paume' makes very similar points to the work on painting, but on theatre. The essays 'Adorno come diavolo' and 'Plusieurs silences' do the same for music and 'Sur une figure du discours' and 'Petite économie libidinale d'un dispositif narratif: la régie Renault raconte le meurtre de P. Overney' the same for discourse.

'La peinture comme dispositif libidinal' begins by distancing its use of desire from the view that the secret of painting lies in uncovering the artist's desire. Painting is not fundamentally the expression of desire, in the same way as it is not fundamentally the expression of Nature as defined by the romantics (see 'La peinture comme dispositif libidinal', DP: 227). Lyotard does not want to reorientate the interpretation of painting to the psychoanalysis of an artist's desires; in fact, he is highly critical of what he sees as a misappropriation of Freud. Instead, desire is a way into matter and affects. These work through a certain understanding of desire and against another. This distinction depends on the now classic distinction in Freud of two ways of understanding desire: desire as desire for something (desire as wish) and desire as unconscious impulse (desire as primary process). It is the latter that is important in painting. Lyotard's works of this period all owe a great debt to this distinction and to a further distinction drawn within desire as process between Eros and the death drive.

Freud's *Beyond the Pleasure Principle* had a profound effect on Lyotard. It is his way of deducing the necessity of a philosophy beyond good and evil as things to be willed directly. He returns to the book again and again in order to insist on the inescapable connection of the two drives and on their role in the affirmation of life. Both drives give energy to a system through the repetition of affects. In the case of Eros, it is a repetition of processes and affects contributing to the internal running of the system (the affect triggered by feeding, or exercise, or sex, or pleasure taken in the confirmation of opinions about beauty or form). In the case of the death drive it is repetition of processes and affects that disturb that good running (a more 'destructive' repetition of a sexual or other practice). So in one case energy is exploited in an orderly fashion through the repetition of process and affect; in the other case energy destroys the system and moves towards something external (229). Under the impulse of the death drive, the system changes and in that sense dies. Under the impulse of Eros the system tends towards stasis and in that sense dies. The search for an active passivity in Lyotard (and Deleuze and Foucault) is a response to the consequent requirement to play off the two drives against one another – strategies for a life between two deaths.

But from the point of view of allowing energy to flow through the system, the death drive is as positive as the energetic stabilisation of Eros. Like Deleuze and Guattari in their *Anti-Oedipus*, Lyotard moves away from any sense of a norm and judgements of value in terms of drives. He refuses to accept that it is possible to isolate some processes and associated affects with negative results. This moves him (and Deleuze and Guattari) away from the healing function of psychoanalysis. It also dissociates him from a politics of health and normality, or indeed a politics of perversion *à la* de Sade (Lyotard's relation to de Sade is, however, not a purely critical one; see *Libidinal Economy*, 89–90). This opposition to the association of psychoanalysis and good practice, norms or a doxa comes out very clearly in Lyotard and Deleuze's strong opposition to the influence of Lacan when this takes on an authoritative bent. This point is repeated throughout *Des Dispositifs pulsionnels* and *Libidinal Economy* (52–66). It takes its strongest political form in a joint statement by Deleuze and Lyotard 'Concerning the Vincennes Psychoanalysis Department' in *Les Temps Modernes* (1975):

> What psychoanalysis presents as its knowledge is accompanied by a kind of intellectual and emotional terrorism that is suitable for breaking down resistances that are said to be unhealthy. It is already disturbing when this operation is carried out between psychoanalysts, or between psychoanalysts and patients, for a certified therapeutic goal. But it is much more disturbing when the same operation seeks to break down resistances of a completely different kind, in a teaching section that declares itself to have no intention of 'looking after' or 'training' psychoanalysts.
>
> (PW: 69)

This statement was in response to a purge initiated in the Vincennes psychoanalysis department 'on the instructions of Dr. Lacan'.

Lyotard claims that when painting is studied in terms of desire, process and affect it immediately becomes a question of political economy as well as libidinal economy. This is because desire works on systems, either to transform or to preserve them. Painting is therefore concerned with political acts in the sense of the metamorphosis of social structures and systems through affects and processes. He speaks of this in terms suited to conflict in politics: thoughts in dreams are 'transformed, adjusted, undone, broken, mended, ground down, crushed into manifest content . . .'. Painting as metamorphosis is the release of affects when gesture sets down and spreads colour on a support. These affects work on systems, on dispositions. Sometimes they prop dispositions up, when they are capable of using the affect and colourful matter. Sometimes they destroy them by 'diluting dispositions and their arrangements of energy, making them go by excess, liquifying them, mixing them up'. In fact, in 'La peinture comme dispositif libidinal', Lyotard insists on the conclusion that the functions cannot be separated: 'at the same time energy as order and disorder, as Eros and death drive, always together' (DP: 231). When a gesture and colour release affects they cannot help taking on a political function of support and disturbance, not only within the rules and canons of the tradition, but in all the systems that these affects can be set to work in. Does this very general definition of painting allow for the precision that was sought earlier in this chapter? Does it allow us to become clearer on what is meant and achieved by active passivity?

Two consequences of the definition do bring us closer to a precise sense of the political as a libidinal active passivity in the context of painting: liberation and experimentation. First, painting is not restricted to a particular social sphere or region. It is not defined by its place within the 'Beaux-Arts'. It cannot be restricted to the intentions or emotions of the painter. Neither should it be thought of in a limited cultural sense, either in the terms of the Marxist definition of superstructure or in a less rigorous association with a particular class function. Theories of painting that limit it to a certain social region and function cannot account for its full libidinal potential in terms of affects and systems or dispositions. So, second, painting is the search for a release from those regions and an extension into new dispositions and new affects.

More precisely, Lyotard speaks of a 'dilution' of pictorial regions. This implies that painting is not so much an escape from its traditional regions and practices as an experimental extension out of these. This extension cannot be primarily theoretical in the sense of a conceptual or dialectical extension of the role of art (a greater political role for its institutions based on the value of culture, or the participation of artists in social debate). Painting, as defined by Lyotard, has neither this conceptual nor dialectical element in the explanation of how it works. It is not defined in terms of social functions or values, but in terms of how it disturbs and supports them libidinally. Painting does not live by what it says or communicates, but by what affects it conducts.

According to Lyotard, the history of modern art is the history of this dilution. It is the search for the extension of the practice of painting (simply, the colouring of something) and its affects (the way it moves us) into wider dispositions and away from tradition: 'there is a polymorphy of modern painting that testifies to an analogous dissolution [to that achieved by capitalism] of the objects, states, configurations, places, modalities that defined the boundaries of the institution we call painting' (DP: 233). Lyotard is able to embrace the techniques of modern painting free of the questions of judgement 'But is this art?', 'But is this beautiful?' and 'But is this responsible?' Instead, an important part of painting and writing on painting is the experimentation with ways of 'making colourful inscriptions' as opposed to making judgements about their value (235). In 'La peinture comme dispositif libidinal' and 'En attendant Guiffrey', Lyotard gives brute materialist accounts of how colour comes to be set down on a support. Anything from drip painting (Pollock) through almost imperceptible shading (Guiffrey) to the application of lipstick is susceptible to his descriptions. The criterion for choosing one practice or another is not in the determination of acceptable and non-acceptable practices in terms of beauty, say. It is in the detection of a transfer of libidinal energy from one disposition (the set-up and affects associated with body-painting – Klein, for example) are conducted into another (our ideas concerning skin, colour, form and matter, say).

The criterion is that of working (is there a transfer?): 'The camera captures luminous energy and inscribes it on film: is it painting? Why ever not? The eye captures the developed and projected photograph, the hand repeats it on a scale of one to ten: is that painting? Many pop and hyper-realist canvases are made this way. It is a disposition, it works' (236). Thus the sense of 'working' here is not utilitarian but energetic, in the sense that intensity revives and displaces systems that tend to inertia (death). A painting works, and indeed any other libidinal political act works, when it releases feelings and desires by extending, clashing and loosening structures.

These acts can be very discreet when compared to great revolutionary movements or creative and destructive pushes. There is no external scale that they can be judged by. It is rather that further acts show that work in a relative pragmatic context by picking up on the movement and intensity released in the first. For example, there could not be a libidinal critical school with a set of criteria and measures for judging the energy of a given art-work. There is intensity and movement – and not a judgement of intensity and movement – where a work (say of philosophy) shifts alongside one that precedes it. So this does not mean that there cannot be movement in critique and judgement. It means that critique and judgement are not the final arbiters of movement. It does not mean that there is no intensity and movement in the desire and structures of final judgements. It means that they are merely one set among many others on which they depend for their intensity.

But does this commit Lyotard to the most banal (and nihilistic) form of relativism? Are there worse and better ways of 'working'? Yes, the more structures are given fixed boundaries and lay claim to final laws, judgements and values, the more any initial intensity released at their creation becomes dissipated and the more opportunities for intensity are resisted. This is the stagnancy and terror that Lyotard seeks to undermine, most notably in the figures of will, self and subject – hence his commitment to active passivity, to 'apathy'.

PAINTING AND APATHY

Thus the 'democratic' aspect of Lyotard's libidinal economics, noted in the previous chapter concerning affects, is repeated in his work on painting. All ways of inscribing colour on a support can count as painting (lines on sand, tattoos). This inclusiveness is one of the key directions for his work on painting and his work as a whole: does this inscription of colour connect this disposition (marks on sand) and its affects to another? Does it breathe new energy into both by intensifying the affect in the transfer? The direction itself allows him to be more precise about how to paint and how to think. Some ways inhibit that extension and maintain inscription in traditional dispositions, thereby leading to a decrease in energy. Others increase energy by conducting the intensity of an affect from one disposition to another. As shown through the work on Freud and the libido, this conduction and positive influx of energy is also destructive in the sense that it disturbs the dispositions. The problem faced by Lyotard and modern painting is how to experiment with colour outside the boundaries of well established rules and traditions. How do we ensure that energy and intensity become universally polymorphous in the sense of flowing through all dispositions?

If Freud is Lyotard's guide in discovering the role of desire in painting, Cézanne points the way to passive experimentation as a means of conducting the affects associated with colour. The problem to be resolved is how to paint free of a dominant disposition and thereby to escape the restriction and eventually the loss of intensity in the affect, since intensity is associated with movement as transformation and destruction. Lyotard approaches the problem in a historical context: the emergence of the disposition of representation in and after the Italian quattrocento (Piero della Francesca, Lorenzetti). The historical dimension of this work – done in detail in *Discours, figure*, then used in *Des Dispositifs pulsionnels* – is important in two

71

ways. First, it shows that the dominance of the disposition of representation is contingent; representation appeared on the scene of painting quite late (Lyotard studies pre-representational religious and primitive art to show this) and therefore cannot be considered the essence of painting (DP: 242–58). Second, it sets the questions 'What is common to different dispositions?' and 'How can this be approached without depending on any particular disposition?'.

We know the answer to the first question to be colour and the intense affect. The answer to the second is passivity. This is described quite poorly in 'La peinture comme dispositif libidinal' in terms of the absence of lines and contours in Cézanne's work. This absence takes away the represented object from the picture and allows colours to affect us directly in the many ways in which they can interact. Lyotard is then able to claim that modern painting is an experimentation into these ways (in Delaunay, for example, we spin from one colour to another). But this account in terms of the absence of contours is unconvincing because of its overly simplistic negative outlook: something has to be taken away for colour to be affirmed. But how is it taken away? Is this elimination the primary process or is it a secondary effect?

These questions are not tackled directly in 'La peinture comme dispositif libidinal' because, there, Lyotard concentrates on the polymorphism of modern painting; that is, on the way in which all possible supports and interactions of colour are investigated. This is to allow the political direction for libidinal economy to emerge as the conduction of intensity into as many dispositions as possible: 'Here, our hypothesis (and belief), based on the movement towards polymorphism in modern painting and economy, has been that the force of what is painted does not lie in its power to refer, to seduce, its "difference", in its status as signifier (or signified), that is, in its lack, but in its fullness of switchable libido' (267). This conclusion, while setting a direction for libidinal economy, does not characterise the way in which that direction can be followed. This work is done in 'En attendant Guiffrey' and 'Freud selon Cézanne' in the descriptions of Cézanne's search for powerlessness and Guiffrey's *apathie*.

Apathy is used here in the non-pejorative Stoical and Spinozist senses of freedom from passions and indifference to desires for specific things (the difficulties involved in this restriction will be looked at below). In Cézanne's work there is a 'mutation of desire' away from the desire to represent an object and even away from the desire for anything outside an arrangement of colours. According to Lyotard in 'Freud selon Cézanne', 'this mutation is not achieved or sought out, but given or, rather, undergone' (DP: 75). It is a factor of what Merleau-Ponty called Cézanne's doubt, an uncertainty that comes from the realisation that there is no law that collects colours in an object. The object is always open to a disintegration into colour and it only appears contingently as a moment between its colourful construction and destruction. This doubt and associated contingency of the object governs his paintings and makes them works of passivity.

When we turn to Merleau-Ponty's 'Le doute de Cézanne', in *Sens et non-sens*, it is striking how many of his intuitions are shared by Lyotard only for the two to be separated on the role of the human. For Merleau-Ponty, doubt is a human factor, something that comes into the world with human freedom. For Lyotard, it is tied to a material factor that underlies the human. This comes out most strongly in their different uses of Freud in interpreting Cézanne. Where Merleau-Ponty uses Freud to approach a necessary doubt or uncertainty in the human condition, Lyotard uses him to explain the transformative power of affects in any disposition. So in the latter the human is a disposition among many and it is subject to an extra-human primary process:

> Cézanne's pictorial journey unfolds in the element of an originary uncertainty, a suspicion with regard to anything that is presented as 'natural law' in the Schools of painting. In the same way, Freud's journey depends upon an initial rejection of the principle of unification of psychic phenomena by consciousness and its replacement by an unsuppressible principle of dispersion (sexuality, primary process, death drive).
>
> (DP: 75)

In the former, existence is revealed in the paradoxical circular freedom of human lives, creating themselves as they really are:

> The hermeneutic reverie of the psychoanalyst, multiplying communications from ourselves to ourselves, takes sexuality for the symbol of existence and existence for the symbol of sexuality. It looks for the sense of the future in the past and the sense of the past in the future. It is better adapted than a rigorous induction to the circular movement of our life that applies its future to its past and its past to its future and where everything symbolises everything.
>
> (Merleau-Ponty 1966: 43)

Lyotard's explanation depends upon a non-human principle that will come to be complicated, though not negated or undermined, in its application in terms of the dissimulation of affects, intensity and dispositions. For him, it is possible to be specific, but not finally, about these factors and processes in any given work. In contrast, Merleau-Ponty depends upon a divided structure of explanation based on symbolisation and therefore on reference (Lyotard's great zero again). Reference is itself then undermined by an infinite multiplication where no final ground or direction is given: 'everything symbolises everything', 'its future to its past and its past to its future'. The only vestige of sense that is allowed to remain is human freedom and its reference to the infinitely postponed identity of a human life: 'Psychoanalysis does not make freedom impossible. It teaches us to think of it concretely as a creative re-take on ourselves. Always true to ourselves after the fact.' But for Lyotard this is the way to nihilism: a fundamental structure of negation raised to infinity and resolved in the religiosity of a forever postponed human identity.

So Cézanne's work and doubt must not be studied with reference to human life or freedom. Instead, Lyotard moves towards the description of processes that allow colour to appear by working against representation. Cézanne's search for powerlessness is a double movement: an active move away from representation and a passivity with regard to the way in which colour will combine and enter into new dispositions. Lyotard speaks of an originary deficiency and relinquishment in the act of painting; that is, to paint free of guiding rules and techniques, allied, though, to a continuous displacement of plastic figures and procedures. This alliance is all-important, not only for Cézanne's painting, but also for Lyotard's politics. Neither is simply a naïve search for vacancy, a pure passivity. Instead, as I have shown towards the end of the previous chapter, there is a conscious and highly elaborate move away from established structures, facilitated by a search for passive moments inscribed within those structures. It is neither a painting or a politics of 'let's empty this space and see what happens', but of 'let's work to loosen and deform this structure by seeking passivity at its most intense points' (colour and form for painting; the subject and representation for politics).

With Cézanne, there is a refusal to allow the work to fit into a pre-established network of exchange, that is, a given set of formulae governing painting. In their place, there is the desire for the painting to be an object in itself, with no outside reference: 'no longer counting as a message, threat, plea, defense, exorcism, morality, allusion, in a symbolic relation, but counting as an absolute object, freed from a transferential relation, indifferent to the relational order, active only in the energetic order, in the silence of bodies' ('Freud selon Cézanne': 85). Passivity is not simply apathy as the absence of desire. It is the desire to work against systems and structures allied to an experimentation that is not conscious and does not seek to be conscious of what it will therefore conduct.

When he talks about Cézanne and Guiffrey, Lyotard therefore insists on the economy of the act of painting in the two senses of a reserve and a process of circulation. In their art there is a holding back of desires, affects and sensations from the temptation of an overblown 'I', their supposed initiator and recipient. In its place we find a set of economic blocks and passages of intensity that remind us of Deleuze and Guattari's economy of flows and cuts developed in *Capitalism and Schizophrenia*, though they never achieve the material quality of Lyotard's treatment: 'caress ranging over the neck: place where the blouse stops, where the skin begins, or indeed the inverse, frontier or fissure? No it is rather the region of transmutation from one skin onto a different skin' (LE: 21). These material 'zones of passage' or 'changes in surface', perceived through libidinal intensities, are the starting-point for his libidinal economic studies. It is essential, once again, to stress their relative status. A passage and a cut can occur any-where, not only as determined by any particular science, but only as a parallel to libidinal intensities. But are the limits of human perception, feelings and desires also limits to this indeterminacy? No, Lyotard is sensi-tive to the way in which art, technology, literature, politics constantly recombine perceptual and sensual limits with desires that have always been polymorphous and perverse; any limit will do and pleasure can be taken in crossing it or in running right up against it.

The combination of a strategy of reserve and an economic description does not commit Lyotard to an art or politics devoid of mechanical com-plexity or difficulty. It means that it is the result of an attempt to create, free of established dispositions, to paint as a body or mechanism and not with consciousness as the history of representation. So the mechanism is at the same time a very difficult turn away from something that is known and a gamble that something else will be conducted. This explains the passion for the process of painting in Lyotard. His works on painting pay special attention to the material steps taken in the execution of the work and how these steps contribute to its libidinal charge at both creation and reception. The state of the artist is deduced from these steps and not the other way round, as would traditionally be the case. So there is not a magic transfer from the artist to the viewer. Rather, there is a common connection to a set of processes, material facts (colour and so on), and wider structures or dispositions (historical, economic, spatial and so on). So the art-work cannot be judged in terms of this transfer, though it is one possible historical disposition. Instead, the art-work is to be studied libidinally in terms of processes, facts and dispositions.

The active part of painting and indeed viewing consists in processes that connect to dispositions and release intensity. Those where Lyotard picks up on the greatest extension and disturbance of dispositions, and hence release, go beyond the painter as subject willing a representation for the viewer. He concentrates on processes that achieve this and to some extent even invents them in the case of Guiffrey. Lyotard uses the neologism *l'efface* (*effacer*: to rub out) to capture the act of rubbing out the painter and the viewer as consciousnesses ('What do I want to do?' 'What is this for me?'). The painter must experiment with ways of painting that forget what has come before and allow affects to enter into new combinations:

> The destruction of composition [in Guiffrey] is that of the *painter-subject*. Guiffrey never *signs* his works, never gives them *titles*, does not keep catalogues. He therefore abolishes himself as their owner.

75

But all his force is dedicated to *leaving the space alone* . . . Painting
is not the painter's expression, there is no painter. Only lines,
surfaces, brilliance, that must be produced as ungraspable.

(DP: 219)

Seek powerlessness. Multiply principles of enunciation. Invite failure.

PASSIVITY AND THE PROBLEM OF COLLABORATION

Lyotard's search for a politics of passivity and disinterest in specific outcomes can seem wildly at odds with his search for a politics that escapes
dominant systems and structures. Perhaps this explains the odd description
of his politics in *Libidinal Economy*: 'Our politics is of flight, primarily, like
our style' (20). How can one flee successfully if the way of escaping is itself a
gamble and necessarily prone to recapture? Why should one even try?
However, one version of this contradiction is relatively unproblematic. The
accusation that this radical openness to future outcomes is perpetually at
risk from a return of structures is one that he would quite happily agree
with. It is the case that a love of contingency and of unconscious processes is
not consistent with guaranteed outcomes of any kind. But it is still a step
away from the rigidity of structures, even if they must return later – a fact
that Lyotard adopts at the core of his philosophy in the concept of
dissimulation.

For him, passivity is the only way of working through structures while
also loosening them and opening them to new combinations, since all other
ways are dependent on structures for the anti-structural outcomes they wish
to lay claim to. None of this would make sense if the concept of dissimulation simply involved the claim that everything is both intensity and
structure or system. But the concept also depends on a set of qualities
concerning the relation of intensity to structure. The relation can be more or
less loose; that is, a structure can be in a more or less fast process of change,
allowing unforeseen intensities to occur and thus structures to appear that
were hidden in the first one. The final outcome of this process is always out
of reach because the relation between structure and intensity is not fixed in
any way. But, as we have seen in the work on art, the point of passivity is
to conduct new unknown and hence unforseen intensities into structures
in order to shift them away from stagnancy and a repressive terror.

The distinction drawn between direct action opening the way for new
intensities to be conducted and indirect outcomes is an important one. It
shows how Lyotard's libidinal philosophy splits any action into what is
actually loosened in given structures and conscious aims. These elements are
in conflict since an action is determined in terms of chosen outcomes by a set

structure (how and what to paint, what the beautiful is, why painting is moral, for example). But this determination is contrary to openness because it seeks to eliminate the necessary unconscious and contingent aspects of experimentation. Intensity cannot be approached directly, if this means consciously; it can only be experimented with by a conscious decision not to aim for specific outcomes. This decision is one that Lyotard wants to extend to all structures and every part of them – hence his attraction to the capacity of modern art to invest any object.

In *Libidinal Economy*, this decision and the standard attack on it are described in terms of the difference between servitude and dependence: 'Stop confusing servitude and dependence. We would like a book of complete dependence: these pieces of the ephemeral patchwork would be composed and added to the body, the fingertips, all over the sheets; and these formations would, for a moment, make us dependent upon them. If there is no cause there is no author' (LE: 261). So in passivity, in the sense of seeking to become a good conductor of intensities, one does not become serf to anything or anyone. That happens when one follows a particular structure; for example, in the way the relation of aim and conscious decision ensnares us in a specific identity and self-consciousness to which we become falsely responsible. Dependence is instead a dependence on the chance occurrence of intensities and the way in which they trigger new configurations of structures (there is no author other than chance).

So Lyotard follows the Spinozist answer to the accusation that with the loss of free will we lose the power to act and the power that goes with action. What we lose – because it does not exist – is the capacity to choose specific outcomes. But what we gain is an understanding of the ways in which we may allow our environment to connect with us and hence increase our power, now redefined as an increase in connectedness, or in Lyotard's case a more polymorphous conduction. This is force as opposed to wilful power: 'So for the last time stop confusing power [*pouvoir*] with force [*puissance*]. If there is labour involved in adding these few instants to the band, it is an elusive powerless labour, which opens up to force. Power is an ego's, it belongs to an instant, force belongs to no-one' (LE: 261). We cannot be serfs to force; only to the illusion of power.

But these answers do little to deflect the accusation that apathy and contingency contribute directly to a specific and particularly nefarious system: capitalism. This contribution is double. It involves the abandonment of the aim to resist and overthrow capitalism that we saw Lyotard drift away from in the last essays on capitalism and that he still wrestles with in some of the essays in *Dérive à partir de Marx et Freud*. This struggle defines a turning-point in his work, where the will to resist capitalism in the name of something else is finally burnt out, to be replaced in *Des Dispositifs pulsionnels* and *Libidinal Economy* by a more affirmative form of political action (albeit affirmation through passivity). This is why Lyotard's preface to the 1994 edition of *Dérive à partir de Marx et Freud* is particularly interesting in insisting on the waning desire to resist while also stressing a new libidinal conception of resistance: the mutual resistance of the unconscious to consciousness: 'Around us people continued to cry: Freedom! we muttered resistance' (10). 'Resistance is a word used by Freud to qualify the opacity that the unconscious opposes to consciousness but also the latter's blindness with regard to the signs of the former.' It is this Freudian sense that the libidinal philosophy exploits to the full. But as we shall see below, this strategy is congruent with capitalism. Is this combination of assent by default and congruence an abandonment of any capacity to resist capitalism or even to define a politics that maintains some distance from the dominance of the rules of markets?

Lyotard asks this question in nearly all of the essays of *Des Dispositifs pulsionnels*. It is an urgent question for two reasons. First, as we have seen in the early essays on Algeria, his work is characterised by an awareness of the power of capitalism to support and even precipitate the most repressive regimes. Second, the act of passive experimentation and the general aim of seeking to conduct intensity as widely as possible are consistent with, even depend upon, capitalism. Thus in his essay on painting as a libidinal disposition, 'La peinture comme dispositif libidinal', Lyotard notes that the polymorphy of modern art, its laudable capacity to give intensity to any object, is 'congruent' with modern capitalism:

> This trait of polymorphy is in deep congruence with the space of modern capitalism. A space in which so-called economic inscription is potentially on anything. There is certainly an extremely precise limit that we call property or law of value. But, potentially, capitalism outlines the possibility of taking anything and putting into circulation under certain minimal conditions . . . There has to be energy in the thing and, if that is the case, it can be metamorphosed into another object, action, affect, whatever.
>
> (DP: 266)

Lyotard's general aim of conducting intensity in all things is mirrored by the capacity of modern capitalism to give value to any object.

This mirroring shows up well in the way pop art elevated everyday objects to the level of art and the parallel way in which, in capitalist societies, the most commonplace objects can become objects of desire and importance. The positive aspects of these processes lie in their extensiveness and ceaselessness. As values become fixed in art and in society, they are overthrown in an energising and liberating 'revolution'. This process knows no bounds and is potentially capable of extending to anything. Art and capitalism are the allies of the liberation of youth from old values, of new sounds and sensations from antiquated structures of artistic merit, of new ways of experiencing the intensity and worth of undervalued or repressed cultures. But, for all the liberating energy afforded by a new movement, there is still always the grafting of capitalist modes of production and hence control on it. There is still the suspicion and often the fact that the demands of the structure have determined the movement from the outset. What loosening and what singular intensities are these? Are they not mere distractions and palliatives that allow a fundamentally unjust system to thrive?

LIBIDINAL ECONOMIES

> . . . it is not true that capitalism does not give us real pleasure in possession [*ne fasse pas jouir*]. It is not true that we should continue to struggle to interpret and transform it as if it were a simple machine of 'alienation', as if it were posited or imposed from the outside as a violation of all desire, as if what supported it were not precisely desire. As if the vast and simple disposition of expanded accumulation, described by Marx, were not a *libidinal* economic disposition, or at least a group of libidinal dispositions.
>
> (*L'assassinat de l'expérience par la peinture, Monory*: 19–22)

Is this not the most craven of reactionary views? Is it not the case that old and deeply unjust powers lie behind the attraction of new and 'valuable' objects and behind the illusory valuation of cultural or other differences? Is it not the case that whenever possessions and desires flow in capitalism they do so on the back of exploitation and alienation? Lyotard attempts to answer these critical questions in chapters III, IV and V of *Libidinal Economy*.

First, Lyotard asks questions of the alternatives and of the theoretical need to posit a possible just society. His belief that there is no privileged region outside the libidinal economy is translated into an attack on the rather simple version of Marxism that depends on the claim that labour cannot be reduced to its exchange-value at the expense of its use-value. Therefore, revolution need not occur in the absence of the crisis that this contradiction ought to have induced in capitalism. The theoretical commitment to a surplus in labour, falsely exploited by capital, is abandoned with the concomitant view that the alienation of workers from what has been produced is eliminable. We saw this commitment begin to become troubled in the last essays on Algeria. It is analysed with great care and finally abandoned in the essay 'La place de l'aliénation dans le retournement marxiste' in *Dérive à partir de Marx et Freud*:

In other words, we cannot hope to raise the 'contradiction' between the law of value and creative force through a mediation. We cannot overcome the 'contradiction' between the upper part of the visible surface (alienated in 'reality') and its lower part by constituting an organisation that has knowledge of the lower (of scientific theory). That 'contradiction' *is not one*. There is no contradiction between real alienation and theoretical truth, in the sense of a Hegelian contradiction that bursts and is resolved, of a substance that becomes subject.

(104)

This explains why no end of theoretical teaching can bring about a revolution that successfully resolves the contradiction – something that Lyotard has sought to explain from Algeria, through May 1968, up to the student revolts on the campus of his university, Nanterre, on the outskirts of Paris, in the early seventies. The tension between force and value, between labour and its exploitation, is an attraction as well as a repulsion. They work within one another and that is the unbreakable relation that he sets himself the task of understanding and then working with in *Libidinal Economy*.

The necessary relation between force and a law of value or equivalences is essential to Lyotard's work on capitalism. Put simply, it comes down to the view that energy must be exploited in structures that end up cancelling it out and that these structures burn out unless they find new energy to exploit. But what are this energy and structure? Why are they necessarily linked? Lyotard does not provide an abstract argument and set of definitions in response to this question, other than his work on the necessity of dissimulation outlined in the previous chapter. Instead, he puts forward a set of practical studies that show energy to be intensity, that is, the intensity of desires and feelings.

The studies show the structure to be a law of equivalence, that is, a way of relating incommensurable things in order to allow for their exchange. Finally, they show – but not definitively – that any advocacy of either a structure free of energy or a structure free of a law of equivalence is bound to fail. In the development of his studies, he shows the success of various stages of capitalism to be an ever-improved capacity to manage the opposite but necessarily entangled requirements of energy and structure. It is important to note that this development is not progress in the sense of an overcoming of problems that could not be handled in earlier stages. Instead, he shows how each stage is related to others in the way aspects of the libidinal economy, of the relation between intensity and structure, are more or less present.

Each of Lyotard's studies considers the functioning of a particular economic practice in terms of how well it works with the tension between the need to establish equivalences and the need to feed the structure. However, given his criticism of Marx, he cannot ascribe the import of energy to an exploitation of something external to it. Instead, economies have that 'outside' at their very core in terms of the necessary structuring of the desires that drive them to expand. According with the concept of dissimulation this necessity is mutual: desires depend on the structures as much as the opposite. It would be wrong therefore to assume that Lyotard defines desire as a new exteriority. The real source of energy is then not some raw material, or labour force, or external world. It is the set of desires that force an economy to incorporate intensities that cannot be reduced to the structures that are necessary to allow for them to be exchanged. This is Lyotard's originality: he sets himself the task of describing the positive economic role of desires and the way in which they are brought into a structure of equivalences.

Through this description he is able to develop his understanding of a politics of the passive conducting of intensity. Economies that manage to maximise opportunities for different desires and for their application to as many things as possible provide us with lessons as to how to be good libidinal economists. The key question is: How do we maximise these opportunities, defined as libidinal intensities, at the expense of the effort to stabilise them in a structure of equivalences? This subversive political aim is essential to the work of *Libidinal Economy*. The book does not stand up as a standard work of economics since it is unoriginal and in fact rather jejune at the level of pure theory. Its method is neither logical analysis nor empirical research, but rather a quasi-historical survey carried out through a reading of a limited number of more or less canonical economic and literary texts.

The most simple economy analysed by Lyotard involves desires expressed in terms of 'need'. To define need as a desire may seem pleonastic, but according to his account need is only one sub-type of desire and in effect an illusory one that depends on an arbitrary determination of the units that are to count as needful. For example, for him there is no reason to value a desire for self-destruction beneath a need for preservation. Need is always political and the result of a strategy responding to an instability between structure and intensity and their dissimulation within one another – there is no original organic or ideal reference point.

The economy that comes out of need is one where certain supposedly natural requirements are given a monetary value so that they may be cancelled or satisfied by an exchange for goods. Money comes to represent a need as something that can be cancelled through an exchange: 'The zero of money is the region of annulation, potential, always possible: I am hungry, I buy, I eat; where there was exteriority of a need and a good, nothing remains (need satisfied, good consumed) but the zero of the money paid, passed into the hands of the seller' (LE: 162). Lyotard applies his concept of the great zero (see Chapter 3 above) to this most simple economy and criticises it for its nihilistic tendency.

Money becomes a great zero that represents desires by defining them as needs and thereby allowing them to be exchanged. But the intensity of desires and feelings is lost in this representation. They move us because they are singular and because they cannot be satisfied or exchanged for anything else. Once we settle for the view that love or lust are simply things that can be cancelled in an exchange, they lose intensity in favour of an endless circulation of money for its own sake:

> But I am not saying that the body that speaks, writes and thinks, does not enjoy, it is a section of the flat body of the pulsions, rather than its charge, instead of taking place in singular intensities, comes to be folded back not only onto the need of the market and the city, but onto the zero where both are centred, onto the zero of money and discourse.
>
> (LE: 162)

With that loss we embark on a nihilistic path to loss of energy defined as desire: 'Nihilism brings this with it: needs, one will say, and therefore the bodies who are supposedly their bearers, needs and their proprietors, the talking mouths, create nothing but ceaseless transition' (163).

The next important economic step is not so much away from this nihilism, but something that retards it. This is a point that returns in all Lyotard's subsequent economic studies in *Libidinal Economy*. Changes in and prior to capitalism can only be seen as efforts to delay the onset of nihilism in an economy within which it necessarily returns. This is due to the requirement that things should be exchangeable and hence measured according to a common scale of value. For example, in a simple structure of needs, what counts as a recognised need is limited by an extra-economic factor such as a moral code that sets internal and external boundaries for the category of need.

An aristocratic or racist or sexist law may forbid some sections of the community from owning or enjoying something whilst those who can have these needs may only satisfy them within well-defined guidelines. Such structures tend towards stasis and to nihilism because the intensity of a desire diminishes once it has been thought of as something that can be satisfied and that has an equal status with other things. For Lyotard, the intensity of a desire lies in its incomparability; it is exactly because a singular drive cannot be related to others that it takes us over and energises us. As soon as it is thought of – rather than sensed – it enters into rational calculation in a way that diverts its special quality as something that occupies us uniquely. The possibility of satisfaction is already one such calculation. The possibility of exchange is another.

But this tendency can be put off and the system can be reinvigorated by extending the notion of need and hence the notion of value to all things. Lyotard claims that this anticipates capitalism in two ways: 'First it extends the possibility of being counted and measured to other segments of the pulsional body-band [intensities as material desires]' (LE: 169). There are new things to need and new things to need them. Second, it becomes necessary to ascribe a value of exchange to all things. Therefore value and the possibility of valuation take on a much greater importance and begin to undermine and replace limit codes. However, this second property is a further step to nihilism because thereby money and the judgement of value take on a general role ('But we will not be free from the great zero for all that, quite the contrary' (181)). This generality accelerates the move away from the intensity of singular desires:

> The comparisons and ratios over the pulsional body will take place by means of money, and so the body will cease to be this impossible landscape swept by libidinal influxes, it will be exchangeable piece by piece, part for part, it is centred on its own zero, it makes itself capable of playing rational games with itself, of simulating invest- ments so as to be able to measure them and work out the most profitable combination.
>
> (LE: 170)

The extension of needs to the point where anything can be given a value and hence where the concept of need becomes redundant, in its sense as basic or natural, is a double-edged process for Lyotard. On the one hand, the move away from fundamental needs illegitimately imposed by an authority is to be welcomed as exactly the kind of loosening and openness that his philosophy advocates. Movement and change become things to be valued as enhancing the economy, while exclusion or marginalisation have the potential to be overturned as value is ascribed to new 'needs' However, the vehicle for this value and the power to ascribe it take on greater importance, thereby reversing or at least threatening any advantage gained.

Lyotard thinks about this paradox in terms of two 'deaths' that run parallel to his treatment of Eros and the death drive in Freud (see above). The economy of generalised needs that turns into an economy for all possible desires still has the nihilistic drive to compare and organise through the setting of monetary value. But it also has a death drive to seek out new and disturbing intensities that are as yet valueless and all the more intense and valuable for that. Desire for something that has no value and therefore something for which one sacrifices oneself is always destined to be given a value in this generalised economy. There can be no intense desire satisfied in our sacrifice without the centralising order making sense

83

of it by ascribing some value and hence re-inscribing it into a cycle of exchangeability:

> But side by side with this useless torching, the Brahmin priest is given a tip. And why is this? Because he who gives without return, must pay. The time of jouissance is bought. The time of his ravaged, broken, jubilant, sacred body is converted into cash (and it is expensive). When the daksina has been paid, then he will recover his organic, unified body, which will be able to start afresh in the closed cycle of exchanges . . .
>
> (LE: 184)

This passage allows us to understand a little further what Lyotard is trying to do in his studies of economic relations. Firstly, he wants to set them alongside other powerful desires and feelings in order to show how they are inseparable: sexual desires are economic and economic desires are like sexual desires: they are about the tension between life and death expressed in the positive and negative aspects of an endless and chaotic series of intensities: fear, revenge, greed, hunger, jealousy . . .

The analogy is important since it allows him to insist on the irrational side of any economy. Any given economic state may be modelled very carefully according to accurate economic theories, but these will never have the last word on the future of that system, since its inclusion of and dependence upon libidinal intensities opens it up to their unpredictable occurrence and to the difficulties of handling them. The desire to achieve equivalence and the desire to satisfy 'needs' are all the stronger because of the way in which they intensify and make possible other less obviously economic desires. This explains why Lyotard concentrates on topics that are usually shied away from: the economics of prostitution, sexual use and perversion. In them we see more clearly what is dissimulated in all exchanges. Secondly, he seeks to show how this dissimulation allows us to understand the so-called contradictions and paradoxes of economic exchange. They occur because of the way in which any economy is a struggle between a tendency to stasis, that is, a purely rational exchange where the most perfect system allows for the most efficient satisfaction of needs, and a tendency to unmeasurable excess, the sacrifice of parts of a system in a desire that cannot be exchanged (an individual or a group taken over by a singular desire, an 'uneconomic' obsession).

For example, in order to resolve the tendency to see economies as simply efficient ways of distributing goods according to needs, and hence of diminishing their intensity and expansion, economies begin to concentrate desires and the concept of need on money itself. Thus Lyotard's study of mercantilism and of the strategy devised for Louis XIV by Colbert shows how they re-intensified economic relationships by introducing the desire to hoard money. Money was allowed to accumulate in France as it cornered as many markets as possible in order to cause a state of lack and hence dependence abroad (this is a libidinal state in craving and the perverse pleasure taken in causing it): 'Thus an "exterior" is formed on the other side of the customs barrier whose only role is to be emptied into an "interior", an enormous transfer of the energies current on the ambiguous body of Europe, fuelling the incandescence of the Versailles feasts' (*Libidinal Economy*: 199).

Again, Lyotard wants to insist on the libidinal quality of this form of economy. It is a matter of jealousy and of the perverse pleasures that can be taken in keeping something only for oneself and then destroying it in front of those one has deprived: 'Such is the jealousy of despotism which fuels mercantilism, this latter could not content itself with taking and destroying, but had to present in itself what it annihilated on the outside' (199). The use of the concept of fuelling is important here because it shows how the analysis is free of negative connotations concerning natural needs and hence natural wastage: jealousy in all its will-to-destroy is libidinally intense and hence valuable. But that is not to say that jealousy does not dissimulate other contradictions. There is no valid meta-theory of feelings and desires that allows us to classify them according to importance, intensity, chains of cause and effect. Mercantilism itself fails because it depends on positing the money supply as limited – hence its dependence on gold and silver. If money could be produced infinitely then there would be no sense in hoarding it. The system is seen to depend on accumulating a limited supply. It must therefore tend to a final limit and exhaustion, but what comes after this exhaustion is contingent and unpredictable in the sense that it will not have finally done with the problems of mercantilism, nor will it stand as a system that is not itself open to new contradictions and occurrences.

MODERN CAPITALISM AND ACTIVE PASSIVITY

Modern capitalism emerges to bury this limit tendency of mercantilism. As ever, it cannot finally overcome it, but it can set it to work alongside other operations and desires in order to control its destructive capacity. Limit tendencies are overcome in modern capitalism through a new understanding of the relation between exchange in terms of equivalences and intensities. This relation changes from an opposition to a mutual benefit: a common interest in an increase in energy. Instead of viewing libidinal intensities as things merely to be exploited and hence finally to be exhausted, they are viewed as things to invest in, in the sense of encouragement with a view to reaping benefits later. For capitalism, anything that can be invested in order to provide an increase in intensity can be brought into a structure of equivalences. There are, therefore, no limits imposed on what can count as having value or on the initial value of a thing. In terms of intensity alone, the external and internal boundaries of capitalism are infinite, though this is not the case once these boundaries have to be subjected to the law of equivalences.

Lyotard does not test this directly on an economic model, but through an interpretation of classical Chinese erotics. This is important because it shows how his concern with Taoism and passivity, noted above in the context of art, is placed alongside an interest in modern capitalism as opposed to distanced from it. A passive politics is not something that moves away from contemporary economics, but towards it. The politics is in no way regressive or nostalgic, if that means a return to an earlier economic model. On the contrary, the greatest opportunities for a passive politics are in modern capitalism. This is also true for art and, indeed, for sexuality and education. This relation and examples of the strategies open for taking its opportunities are studied at great length in his work on the painter Jacques Monory. Indeed, in this libidinal period Lyotard often argues that art is political in a wider sense precisely because it is libidinal like every other disposition or set-up that can be worked within capitalism.

This does not mean, though, that these opportunities are easy to take or that they can be taken once and for all – in the sense of a final move with no return. On the contrary, Lyotard seeks out an ongoing and difficult strategy to overcome a set of problems that have been outlined in his work on economics and that culminate in the duplicitous capacity of modern capitalism to invest in intensities while also delaying their actual occurrence. This delay is doubly problematic for Lyotard. Not only does it mean that money continues to take priority over singular material desires through the new desire to see their monetary value increase over time. Now the value of all things is counted in terms of growth potential over time. But also a new and typically capitalist duo of libidinal figures take on great importance: the desire to delay pleasure being taken in something and the desire to be delayed in taking pleasure in something.

When taken to a 'perverted' limit (which is exactly what he wants to do), these figures explain the importance taken by sado-masochism in *Libidinal Economy*. It is not a simple shock tactic or interest in transgressive and hence liberating sex. It is rather that the desires involved are characteristic of capitalist relations to money and to intensity. The task that Lyotard sets himself in relation to this association of money, time and intensity is how to exploit the capacity to intensify desires while resisting their nihilistic funnelling into the mere relation of time and money. His study splits into two at this point: he attempts to investigate the relation of time, money and intensities further to show, not its contradictions, but its nihilistic tendencies. But he also looks at the different ways in which a properly libidinal politics can work within capitalism to affirm intensity despite this trend to nihilism.

Taoist erotics are close to capitalism through the tension involved in the desire to give as much pleasure as possible to a partner, but only in order to gain benefit from it: 'In Taoist erotics, the arrangement is such that it will operate in such a way as to arouse in the woman, by meticulous analysis and consideration of the postures and procedures proper to the maximisation of *jouissance*, the intense excitement of her *Yin* energy, with a view to stealing it from her' (LE: 202). Sex is a struggle between two partners who spend and risk energy for a greater return later. Each one is playing a tight game with time, trying to delay time where it benefits their goals and to accelerate where it benefits the other's. This conflict is the source of the intensification of pleasure through the strategies used to delay and to exploit: 'What the woman gives leads to an agonizing struggle and the cry, by means of the innumerable outflows of liquids described in the Treatises, which is nothing more than her water [*Yin*] which has been shaken up so much; and this is why the man, who is on the *Yang* side, will be able to be enriched by seizing it' (204).

The incommensurability of riches, *Yin* and *Yang*, is crucial here because it forbids a zero-sum game and hence a resolution that calculates the maximum common benefit available to all partners. Lyotard is critical of game theory throughout *Libidinal Economy* because he believes that a game is misunderstood when its stakes are analysed according to a single measure (173–7). This is also why it would be a mistake to theorise sex as a simple collaboration ('let's follow this strategy together for mutual benefit'). First, this would be to reduce the intensity of the act by moving to a plane of consciousness and calculation. Second, that calculation would have to assume that the feelings and desires at play were commensurable. According to Taoist erotics, the man seeks to reserve semen in order to obtain the best possible return in terms of children, while the woman attempts to make the man come in order to weaken his resistance to her attractive forces. The less semen expended, the more numerous and healthy the children. So the man tries not to give himself to the woman by treating her as a means while she attempts to draw him in and to become an end. It is only from this tension of incommensurable drives that pleasure is intensified.

From the point of view of libidinal economics, this tension has a nihilist but also an affirmative component. It is nihilist in the turn towards rational calculation and in the move away from libidinal intensity towards the stocking of an abstract value (children, a dynasty). But it is affirmative in the way in which the strategy for achieving this stock depends on an intensification of pleasures and desires. This opposition is characterised further by Lyotard in terms of a nihilist move towards the subject, possessor of reserves and desiring future stocks (my dynasty, my semen), and an 'anonymous' set of techniques and body parts that can be tools and locations for intensity. Rules and codes no longer govern desires, sensations and where they can be taken. They govern the way intensity is preserved: 'The rule is no longer a line passing around the field where what must happen indeed takes place, while excluding what must not take place . . . it serves to do nothing more than to engender, by the impossibility of situating the act in relation towards it, this non-place or this unthinkable place which is precisely the passage of intensity' (LE: 206).

This explains why capitalism is an opportunity and an ally for the politics of libidinal economy. It is no longer only a question of having to break and transgress rules that forbid this or exclude that. It is no longer only a question of attempting to go beyond a set of internal limit tendencies. It is rather a question of exploiting the drive towards anonymous and neutral intensities that is essential to the capitalist rule of increasing intensity. The principles guiding Lyotard's passive politics outlined in the previous chapter (seek powerlessness, multiply principles, invite failure) and explained further as an active experimentation with passivity and apathy are, then, not only consistent with the affirmative aspect of capitalism; they also affirm it against the tendency towards nihilism involved in the last rule of the stocking of intensity.

The capitalist rule dissimulates intensity and intensity is dissimulated in the rule. The properly economic argument for this concerns a translation of the problem of deflation and inflation into a libidinal account. The former occurs because of the tendency of capitalism to reduce return on investment by struggling to eliminate speculative opportunities through the law of equivalence. This diminishes the intensity that can flow into the system. The latter occurs when speculative movements gain too much power and the law of equivalence cannot be upheld in money. This then leads to hyperinflation. Lyotard goes into some depth in terms of an account of the different roles that can be taken by money (something that sets equivalences, something that allows for borrowing time, something that is a source of speculative greed and envy) in order to show that one can never have done with any one of them. Therefore we cannot dream of a perfectly stable capitalism; neither can we define it as something terminally unstable. It is rather another case of the unstable dissimulation of intensities in structures or dispositions. This means that the idea of the political best suited to opening the structure up is still that of active passivity.

In no way, though, does this imply that we must no longer think and act in terms of traditional politics and economics. Given political and economic systems and theories handle libidinal intensities and will fail to handle others. They are the structures within which a political strategy of active passivity must take place. But no one of them, with its aims, categories, programmes and solutions, must be taken as the right or final one. In fact, active passivity must be deployed to counter that idea and its apparent truth. So the key critical question is not: 'Is Lyotard an absurd revolutionary, seeking to move away from forms of thought and action that we know to be at least relatively true?' He wants to remind us of that relativity and, indeed, to encourage it. Instead, the key question is 'Is Lyotard lacking in judgement when he advocates a political strategy of opening the way to unforeseeable events as the solution to nihilism?' This is the question that must be answered in the following and the final chapters.

5

THE TURN TO JUDGEMENT

QUESTIONS OF JUDGEMENT

It is common to view Lyotard's work in its entirety as an attempt to argue for a special role for events or unpredictable occurrences. Their function is two-fold. First, events prevent illusory applications of types of judgement to things that necessarily exceed their proper field. Second, events defined as limits to knowledge demand the greatest attention in art, philosophy and politics. These disciplines are in fact intertwined in their relation to events. Thus, as we have seen, Lyotard's libidinal philosophy investigates the disruptive effect of intensities on dispositions, defined respectively as unpredictable events and any structure organised according to a unifying set of rules or laws. The libidinal politics then goes on to advocate experimentation with ways of encouraging the occurrence of intensities and the extension of different dispositions into one another through the disruptive capacity of events. Modern art is one form of this experimentation. Thanks to it, and to a study of Far Eastern texts and theatre, Lyotard begins to sketch a set of principles for this experimentation. I have singled these out and argued that they provide the key for a consistent and exciting development of his libidinal philosophy and politics of active passivity. This is itself a move out of an impasse that he is seen to go down in the early works on Algeria and in some of the later texts on Marx and Freud.

However, I have also argued that there is a break in Lyotard's work between libidinal economics and the philosophy of the differend. For example, though they share a desire to oppose terror, the means for doing so are very different. In the libidinal works this takes place through a strategy of flight: terror is undermined by an indirect release of desires and feelings that affirm what terror seeks to eliminate. We flee into intensities of desire and feeling and that undermines structures that lead to terror through the imposition of fixed categories and set laws. This undermining, though, is purely chance-driven as to its success with regard specific targets. Something will be undermined, but when and how and with what consequences is open to chance. The effect of undermining something precise is not therefore an aim of a libidinal politics. In the later works regarding the philosophy of the differend, a strategy of direct resistance comes to the fore: testify to irresolvable differences by arousing and listening to the feeling of the sublime.

There is experimentation and art in both positions. The feeling of the sublime is primarily aesthetic. Lyotard works on it best in his studies of Kant's *Third Critique* and late political writings and of the American abstract expressionist, Barnett Newman. The feeling of the sublime, a conjunction of pleasure and pain, is released and allowed to indicate irresolvable differences. A politics of the differend creates new idioms that allow for the difference to be made clear:

> This is when human beings who thought they could use language as an instrument of communication learn through the feeling of pain which accompanies silence (and of pleasure which accompanies the invention of a new idiom), that they are summoned by language, not to augment to their profit the quantity of information communicable through existing idioms, but to recognize that what remains to be phrased exceeds what they can presently phrase, and that they must be allowed to institute idioms which do not already exist.
>
> (TD: 13)

For example, the feeling of the sublime may call us to think about sexuality in order to be able to show how different sexes are incommensurable, that is, have no common measure whereby their difference can be eliminated or sublated. This does not mean that we must create a new common language. Rather, it means that where the dominance of a single one hides a difference, a new idiom must come and sit alongside the first in such a way as to be impossible to absorb. A supposedly continuous range of values (strong–weak, normal–abnormal, stable–mad) may hold sway over a field that the feeling of the sublime drives us to experience as irreconcilably differentiated. This absolute difference is a differend: 'The differend is the unstable state of language wherein something which must be able to be put into language cannot yet be' (TD: 13). A politics of the differend is one that participates in political debate by creating a new idiom for one different part in order to show the illegitimacy of the continuous valuation – not so much abnormal or weak as opposed to normal and strong, but irreducibly different and valuable as such. Lyotard does not define this politics as a universal responsibility or obligation, or in terms of a general political state. Instead, it is something that defines a particular calling proper to certain creative acts: 'What is a stake in a literature, in a philosophy, in a politics perhaps, is to bear witness to differends' (13). If there is to be a politics of the differend, it will be in this giving voice to an excluded party, but without allowing it simply to become part of a wider system of justice. On the contrary, the new voice should disable a common justice of resolutions and shared values.

So what is the main opposition between the libidinal philosophy and the philosophy of the differend if it concerns neither means (experimentation), nor central field (events), nor even the end result (difference affirmed at the expense of illegitimate systematisation)? The answer lies in different interpretations of this end and in its status within the means and field. In the libidinal politics, the end can only be referred to as that which may occur when that politics is pursued. It is neither its direct goal nor something intrinsic to the political act (in the sense of cause and effect, for example). So, in this case, experimentation is never a matter of affirming differences or seeking to oppose systems. Furthermore, what is to count as an event is not defined by radical differences and, indeed, cannot be selected according to a felt difference. On the contrary, an event is a singular attraction that occurs in an aleatory fashion and that can only be invited through active passivity. We cannot consciously select where we are going and what vehicle will take us there. Indeed, any event may do with no prejudice as to its form. So there can be no privileging of radical differences either at the level of event or at the level of goal. This does not mean that differences cannot be in play. They are necessarily, since an intensity occurs where structures clash. But how and where they are to clash we cannot know. In fact, the only radical difference at play in this scenario is that of the unpredictability of the relation of intensity and structure. In the libidinal philosophy, incommensurability lies in the relation of intensity and structure.

In the philosophy of the differend the end serves as a conscious goal for experimentation: act so as to testify to absolute limits. This end also determines the field of events: events occur with a differend, that is, on the border of incommensurable genres. Lyotard defines genres by a set of laws that govern the way in which we must link on from a given event; these laws then determine what he calls the stakes of the genre, for example, knowledge, the good or the beautiful. So each genre is known through the set of laws that determine what is an appropriate reaction to a given occurrence in terms of an overall stake. Incommensurable genres thus have radically different stakes: 'In this sense, a phrase that comes along is put into play within a conflict between genres of discourse. This conflict is a differend since the success (or the validation) proper to one genre is not the one proper to others . . . The multiplicity of stakes, on a par with the multiplicity of genres, turns every linkage into a kind of "victory" of one of them over the others' (TD: 136).

This seems to involve Lyotard in a rather simple 'performative contradiction', easily flushed out with the question: 'Is not the language used to describe all the different stakes a basis for reconciling radical differences?' The sublime is a solution to the contradiction in so far as the final determinant of limits between genres is the feeling of the sublime and not some transcendent discourse. Thus, if we are to interpret this position in terms of the libidinal philosophy, we note that intensities – the feelings of pleasure and pain combined in the feeling of the sublime – are signs of a politically more important event: a differend or incommensurability of genres.

This solution is omitted from some of the first stabs at a philosophy of the differend in *The Postmodern Condition*. Notwithstanding the book's prominence and influence, I will steer clear of it. It has an illegitimate stature within Lyotard's work and in debates on the postmodern, due to its ease of access when compared to his other much more consistent and deep books. It is a small irony, but no comfort, that the postmodern effect of rapid dissemination of shallow but fashionable ideas and debates has led to the ugly combination of fame and easy dismissal in the reception of the book. The sooner it reverts to the background position of something like a discussion paper the better. This position is also backed by Lyotard in his interview with Van Reijen and Veerman, 'Les lumières, le sublime', *Les cahiers de philosophie: Jean-François Lyotard, réécrire la modernité*, 63–98, esp. 64. This is not to give any great weight to his self-evaluation, or indeed to the simplifications that tend to occur with interviews, but merely to point to a further reference that may be of some interest. Unlike *The Postmodern Condition*, *The Differend* uses an elliptic style as well as the juxtaposition of different types of discourse in order to escape a reduction to the simple transcendent account outlined above. In this chapter, the later book will be my main reference in conjunction with Lyotard's work on Kant and the sublime.

However, having drawn a distinction between Lyotard's libidinal work and his philosophy of the differend, it is important to note how the introduction of the feeling of the sublime affects it. The difference between two relations to political ends becomes much smaller when seen from the point of view of sublime events, since these are sensual intimations of the limits of all ways of achieving ends that involve bridging a differend. This is best seen in the paradoxical statements from *The Differend* that combine the necessity to follow on from events with the stake of not following according to a rule or law that assumes that the event can be finally understood or categorised. We feel that an event has occurred, that we are faced with a differend, and the feeling defines our action in terms of a negative stance with respect to bridging laws and rules. In other words, we feel that laws and rules that allow us to act in such a way that we fix the event or resolve the difference are illegitimate. So the sublime event is something that grabs us so strongly that any of our acts 'follow on from it' – even the act of trying to pretend it did not happen – this is its necessity. It is also, though, an event that makes us aware of the redundancy of resolutions according to laws and rules. In that sense it defines a paradoxical rule for the political, philosophical and artistic resistance: 'to create our necessary reaction as if it could not be subsumed under bridging laws and rules'.

For example, the silence of victims who are incapable of expressing the wrong done to them can be a sublime event in Lyotard's sense: 'Silence as a phrase. The expectant wait of the *Is it happening?* as silence. Feelings as a phrase for what cannot now be phrased. The immediate incommunicability of desire, or the immediate incommunicability of murder. The phrase of love or the phrase of death' (TD: 70). In his philosophy of language any event can be thought of as a phrase, including silence. In this case, silence is a phrase accompanied by a sublime feeling that something needs to be put into a phrase of understanding, that is, a cognitive phrase. But this is exactly what cannot happen if we remain within the boundaries of understanding defined as knowledge of (another's desire, love, pain, death).

So it seems at this point that any phrase can be an event in the sense of calling us to search for a new and ultimately impossible way of expressing the differend between a given definition of knowledge and a 'fact' that cannot be comprehended according to that definition. Clearly, this discussion intersects with Wittgenstein's philosophy, notably with his reflection on the impossibility of private languages and his remarks on pain. A study of this relation would be valuable since Lyotard is strongly influenced by Wittgenstein, not only in the idea of language games, but more significantly perhaps in his later work on the role of rules and laws. However, I will not pursue this matter here, preferring instead to concentrate on politics and the question of judgement in Lyotard's reading of Kant. This approach is justifiable through the more overt political links and the more in-depth and precise treatment of Kant by Lyotard. Lyotard's philosophy of language has been studied and criticised at greater length in my *Lyotard: Towards a Postmodern Philosophy* (1998: 62–89).

My use of 'impossible' in describing the task of a politics of the differend should not be taken as a sign of a straightforward logical contradiction at the heart of Lyotard's philosophy of language. It is used to point to the combination of the necessity of a response together with its ultimate failure, if success is to be defined as bridging the differend once and for all. That cannot happen and, instead, our political act that testifies to the differend shows this impossibility by expressing one side of the differend. I put the desire, pain, love into a genre that makes the clash with the genre of knowledge apparent. This then avoids the particular injustice of assuming that silence is a wilful or obtuse failure to communicate. It also avoids the general terror of assuming that communication is ultimately always possible in a given genre. Impossibility may then become something blameworthy upon which a given genre has the right to draw its own conclusions.

However, if any phrase can be a sublime event, are we not approaching the inclusiveness and passive attitude to intensity from the libidinal philosophy outlined and defended in earlier chapters? This is not the case for two very important reasons. The first concerns a restriction as to what can count as intensity, or more precisely, as to what can count as politically significant intensity. The second concerns the nature of this signification: the sublime is a sign of a differend. As an intensity, the feeling of the sublime is an incapacity or limit caused by the conjunction of two opposed intensities (pleasure and pain; expectancy and fear). The opposition makes it impossible for one of the intensities to drive us into a new singular attraction and new structures, in the way it would occur in love or desire, for example. Instead, we are driven back into the incapacity and what it signifies: the differend or absolute difference. This does not mean that we are simply rendered incapable of any action, but rather that the only possible action is the search for ways of testifying to the differend. If we are driven by the sublime, we cannot think our way into incapacity and nihilism because the primary event is already a drive to act; hence the combination of pleasure and pain, expectancy and fear.

The definition of a sublime event as limit also explains why Lyotard is able to claim that the sublime event is not a sign as understood in structuralism. I have called it so, following Lyotard, because of the relation between the sublime and the differend: the former indicates the latter. But this does not imply that any particular sublime event is a signifier of a particular positive thing, of a signified that can be comprehended and structured in a relation to other signifieds. The sublime does not contribute to a structure of meanings that underlie a structure of sensations. It inhibits both those structures by standing out as a privileged event. It cannot be recuperated as a sensation among others since it cannot be compared through the medium of what it signifies.

There is no such medium because the sublime is a 'sign' that any structure of signifieds and overarching meaning is an illusory bridge between absolute differences. So there is nothing to be decoded in the sublime due to the absence of a possible code or set of underlying relations; there is only a differend, an absolute difference that cannot be read and understood. Thus we have the paradox of a sign that indicates an impossible passage or, better, makes us feel that impossibility. At times, Lyotard is averse even to describing this as a sign since he wants to insist that the sublime has no meaning. Quite the contrary; it is a feeling that there can be no meaning and that this must be testified to: 'But the occurrence [event] doesn't make a story, does it? – Indeed, it's not a sign' (TD: 181).

So there is no real openness to all events in the philosophy of the differend. There is a hierarchy where the political concerns only differends associated with the feeling of the sublime. This could not be further from libidinal economics, where active passivity cannot involve such selectivity in terms of intensities and in terms of the systems within which they may occur. The former has a powerful sadness at its heart in the feeling of the sublime, where the pleasure of acting for an injustice is shackled to the pain of feeling that there can be no resolution. The latter, on the other hand, seems to suffer from an incapacity to respond to the claim that certain events demand our attention more than others. Neither position leads to an incapacity to act, or indeed to respond to a particular injustice; in both we are driven to do just that and we should seek to be so driven. Neither makes the claim to be able to respond equally to all cases of injustice; we have to be called to them through libidinal intensities or the feeling of the sublime. However, there is a much more restricted range of feelings that prompt political action in the case of the differend when compared to the libidinal economics.

In this sense there is a two-fold lack of judgement in the libidinal philosophy. First, there is a search for an undiscriminating openness at the level of which intensities may flow through us as the result of active passivity. This does not mean that this is itself undiscriminating. As I have shown in the previous chapters, there is an active and careful work against dominant and repressive structures in order to allow for passivity with respect to intensities. Second, there is a lack of judgement with respect to intensities once they have occurred. One does not seek to eliminate or repress an intensity; on the contrary, it is to be encouraged precisely because it has a subversive effect on dominant structures, including those that may allow us to make wise and just selections.

However, this does not mean that Lyotard advocates an abandonment to the passions and to the senses. Dissimulation and the necessary association of intensities with the active strategies that let them flow means that one can never have done with structure or with the ongoing need to develop and work with a given strategy. The libidinal philosophy is far removed from a hyperaesthetic position; it is in fact very precise and complex because of the sensitivity of the relation between given structures, acts designed to loosen them, and the appearance of new intensities (that open the field for further complex work). Therefore one can never have done with judgement in the sense of a refinement of strategies and in the sense of practical experience – so long as we remember that this experience is fragile and subject to revolutions.

So problems concerning judgement cannot be escaped either in *Libidinal Economy* or *The Differend*. Both books involve arguments against familiar and important uses of judgement. Yet they differ in the degree to which they flee it or reserve it for a privileged realm. In the remainder of this chapter, I will seek to resolve some of the problems associated with these stances with respect to judgement through a discussion of Lyotard's *Just Gaming*, in the case of *Libidinal Economy*, and through a discussion of Lyotard's reading of Kant, in the case of *The Differend*. The main questions guiding this chapter will therefore be the following.

1   It seems that a libidinal politics cannot choose its adversaries or its allies. It is incapable of categorising groups, bodies and actions into good and bad, except through the minimal 'choice' of following a chance-driven

path. Is this lack of discriminating judgement in *Libidinal Economy* a sign of the book's political redundancy?

2   *Libidinal Economy* appears to defend a double political coldness or cruelty. On the one hand, it affirms that our struggles must choose us. This means that justice cannot be universal and that causes are fought for on the basis of chance and relative intensity rather than on universal merit. Does a libidinal politics lead to a parochialism, where claims that would be deemed just from the point of view of a universal justice have no right to expect our attention or care?

3   On the other hand, once we have been chosen by a struggle, the question of whether it is a just one has no place. Is Lyotard's libidinal philosophy a basis for a defence of any political action so long as it is associated with intensities and with the clash and distortion of structures?

4   In the philosophy of the differend, is Lyotard right to restrict the field of the most just philosophical and political judgement to differends?

5   Given this restriction and the absolute nature of the difference between genres caught up in a differend, is the resulting philosophy and politics viable? This problem comes out most clearly in the constant return to paradoxes in Lyotard's treatment of the differend. For example, is it possible to say anything positive at all about a differend? Is a stake that guides us to create as if our action could not be subsumed under laws and rules one that finally reduces us to quietism?

6   Does this stake allow for the development of a particularly just genre of philosophy and politics? Or does something other than a well-defined genre or practice emerge? How can this other thing be anything positive and consistent at all given its lack of guidance in the form of laws and rules?

THE NEED FOR JUDGEMENT

> It is not true that the search for intensities or like things is a political matter, because of the problem of injustice.
>
> (Lyotard 1979a: 171)

Judgement begins to become an overt problem for Lyotard in *Au Juste* (1979). In the book, Lyotard is asked a series of questions about libidinal philosophy by a young philosopher, Jean-Loup Thébaud. The main thrust of these questions is towards ethical judgement and political responsibility. The first remarkable aspect of the responses is that they accept the pertinence of the questions. That is, Lyotard does not answer with an attack on the demand for judgement, categories, criteria from the point of view of the libidinal investments that underlie them. Why do you desire judgement?

Why is the desire for judgement to be valued above others? Is judgement an appropriate response to a politics of becoming a good conductor of intensities?

In other words, we might have expected – but we never get – a response along the following lines: Judgement is dependent on a particular type of structure and libidinal investment. It is therefore repressive of other investments and reactive with regard to other possible structures. Judgement sets up oppositions between judge and case, between cases, between laws, between lawful and lawless and so on. None of these is to be desired above any other. Besides, the task of a politics of passive activity is to flee the fixed nature of this structure and thereby to loosen it and open it to new possibilities. So judgement indicates a doubly negative thought, that is, with respect to external possibilities and with respect to internal modes of thought and sensation. In this sense, it is nihilistic. Priority given to judgement runs counter to the active, affirmative, search for passivity. Experimentation must take place free of conscious judgement even if it is always dissimulated in the structures from which it flees and towards which it is drawn; so in *Libidinal Economy* we find a much more robust riposte to demands for judgements based on theory: 'Reply with questions, tell them: and your theoretical discourse, what is it? All your questions have the underlying reference to this discourse, this true speech' (LE: 241).

But in *Au Juste* this attack never takes place. Instead, there is a quite different counter, based around the project of a minimal judgement that owes nothing to set laws and categories. This owes much more to the burgeoning philosophy of the differend than to the libidinal work. Judgement is to be a sensitivity to and response to differences without resort to a pre-set framework for establishing those differences or a belief in the possibility of resolving them: 'Absolutely, I judge. But if I am asked for the criteria of my judgement, I will obviously have no answer. Since if I had such criteria, if I could answer your question, this would mean that there was effectively a possible consensus over criteria between myself and my readers. We would then not be in a modern situation, but in classicism' (*Au Juste*: 32).

In *Au Juste*, Lyotard's answers are couched in terms of a defence of 'paganism', a term that he develops in *Instructions païennes* (1977a) and *Rudiments païens* (1977b), but that begins with *Libidinal Economy*. However, the expression returns in *The Differend* (116), as does a discussion of Cashinahua pagan story-telling (*Au Juste*: 63–71; *The Differend*: 152–5). In *Libidinal Economy*, *the* pagan – and not paganism – is discussed mainly in the section on 'pagan theatrics', where Lyotard draws a distinction between religious theatrics or set-ups, taken from Augustine, and pagan theatrics taken from Varro. The former are said to depend on the reference to one God absent from this world, while the latter multiply gods around each worldly encounter in order to mark its intensity: 'And for each connection, a divine name, for each cry, intensity and multiplication brought about by experiences both expected and unexpected, a little god a little goddess, which has the appearance of being useless when one looks at it with globulous, sad, platonic eyes, which in fact is of no *use*, but which is a name for the passage of emotions' (LE: 8).

In contrast to the fundamental negation at the heart of Augustine's account, pagan theatrics are a strategy for affirming intensities and for avoiding negation by naming the different desires that clash in the intensity. They eschew judgement since it depends on the affirmation of whatever occurs ('a divine name for each cry') and since the cries it affirms are themselves never to be judged (the gods are 'of no *use*'). Augustine's God allows for a referral of each act outside itself, but this use and judgement do not take place in pagan theatrics. So, here, the pagan is a case of a libidinal economic political strategy.

If we take this version of the pagan, Lyotard's answer to the questions concerning judgement outlined in the previous section (questions 1–3) become:

1   A libidinal politics is not redundant, in the sense of lacking the possibility of a chosen direction, since its direction is to affirm what occurs and to draw out its intensity. This does mean that specific directions cannot be selected, but that already presumes a structure of choice and domination over events ignorant and repressive of the deeper liberating power of intensities. The politics of active passivity is a choice for the liberating power of intensities and against the illusion that a 'free' political decision for or against a given case is just or even possible in itself.

2   Yes, a libidinal politics is parochial, in the sense of having to work with a given set of events and, indeed, of affirming that necessity. But this 'working with' is not parochial at all, in a conservative and reactionary sense. First, there is no necessary limit as to our 'parish': it can extend far and wide according to the intensities that we conduct and the structures that regulate them. Second, what occurs can only be affirmed by experimentation. The event must itself be loosened and opened up. Lyotard makes this point again in *Au Juste* in terms of a careful analysis of the strong relation between tradition and paganism. The latter is not a mimetic relation to the past – a conservative tradition – but it is a transformative relation that insists that we can only work properly with a past that makes us and gives us our strength (66–9). However, this is only a last flicker of his libidinal impulses: even as he makes this point Lyotard defines transformation as an act of judgement.

3   When an intensity passes through us, there is no point in asking whether it is just or unjust. It is passing and will pass. So does this mean that where there is pain we must simply accept it? Yes, and more: we must also accept

that there is desire for pain and that pain is an intensity, that is, something powerful against fixed structures and for their extension and deformation. But that does not mean that we must be passive with respect to cruelty and violence as things that we are involved in and subject to. When they are the result of the intolerance of structures with respect to others and to incompatible intensities, cruelty and violence are constantly and actively resisted by a libidinal politics that seeks to release what they dissimulate.

This is the distinction in Lyotard's libidinal philosophy that gives rise to questions concerning judgement and cruelty. It actively seeks to eliminate them where they are the result of static and exclusive structures, while refusing to make judgements with regard to the release of new intensities of pain and new cruel structures in that elimination. It is a politics that takes on the challenge of combating a structural cruelty, so long as it is indicated by an intensity that 'chooses us', but it is also a politics that cannot accept the responsibility of using judgement to construct a new structure free of cruelty. This explains why the section on pagan theatrics in *Libidinal Economy* balks at the possibility of a libidinal politics where there would be no cruel structures: 'Our danger, we libidinal economists, lies in building a new morality with this consolation, of proclaiming and broadcasting that the libidinal band is good, that the circulation of affects is joyful, . . ., that all pain is reactionary and conceals the poison of a formation issuing from the great Zero . . .' (LE: 11). Lyotard's embarrassment with regard to the 'desperation' of *Libidinal Economy*, discussed in Chapter 3, can be put down to an about-turn on the necessity of cruelty implied by the concept of dissimulation.

In *Au Juste*, Lyotard allows the discussion to shift to pagan*ism*, now characterised and defended primarily as a 'way of judging without criteria'. This is a shocking reversal since in his former uses of the term there is no judgement except in terms of how to allow intensities to occur and then how best to affirm them. But, in the later use, judgement occurs first, making a mockery of the earlier priority given to the active search for passivity. Paganism designates 'precisely a situation where one judges. One judges not only in matters of truth, but also in matters of beauty (aesthetic efficacy) and justice, that is, politics and ethics, without criteria' (*Au Juste*: 33). It may appear that there is very little difference here, if we take Lyotard to mean that a pagan strategy is designed to allow intensities to be affirmed and structures to alter, and that this is what is meant by judging without criteria. But this is not the case at all, since throughout the book judgement without criteria is seen as something active that is aided or directed by intensities. It is not a mere by-product that happens to be 'without criteria' because of the nature of the politics of seeking to be a good conductor of intensities. Instead, in *Au Juste* the problem is how to develop 'a capacity to judge' without criteria (36).

The reversal that has taken place can be explained by a further set of questions put by Thébaud and accepted by Lyotard as essential questions. Each question is a problem for a philosophy with judgement at its core:

1   What is the relation between the idea of a judgement 'without criteria' and knowledge? Knowledge is a field where judgement proceeds according to criteria such as 'Does this statement accord with the facts?' Is judgement without criteria then restricted to a fictitious field of metaphysical speculation?

2   Even if the field of judgement without criteria is that of ethics as opposed to knowledge, that is, if it is a field whose objects cannot be shown, but that have a different and important ideal reality, is it not the case that the objects of ethics are exactly laws that we are obliged to follow? So is it not true that judgement in ethics has criteria defined by obligation and by the form of laws?

3   Does not politics presuppose a political community? There must be a community defined either by interest and hence by cognitive judgements as to what is best for the community in a given case, or by a shared set of ethical laws that are either prescribed or to which members of the community are in a position of obligation? The necessity of community for politics is therefore a source of criteria for political judgement.

Lyotard's answers to these questions rest on interpretations of a wide range of philosophers, notably Aristotle, Plato, Nietzsche and Levinas. However, by far the most important and most surprising reference is Kant. His work had appeared very little in Lyotard's books up until *Au Juste* (there are only very brief remarks in *Libidinal Economy* and there is some discussion of Kant on space in *Les Transformateurs Duchamp*: 78–9). In the discussion with Thébaud, he becomes the main source for critical questions against Lyotard's position, but also for a possible answer to them. This answer never really comes in *Au Juste*. Instead, we are given a series of rather hermetic and evasive denials and reiterations. This is explained explicitly in terms of Lyotard's then unresolved relation to Kant: 'To simplify, I am hesitating between two positions, whilst still hoping that this is in vain and that they are not *two* positions. In short, the hesitation is between a pagan position, in the sense of sophistry, and let's say a Kantian position' (141). Lyotard is deluding himself here. His hesitation is not meaningful since the book has already incorporated a Kantian framework for the discussion. The real problem that Lyotard's philosophy has become involved in is whether Kant's philosophy can be interpreted in such a way as to allow for judgement to replace the 'cruelty' of the libidinal philosophy but without having to commit Lyotard to a politics based on Kantian conceptions of knowledge, obligation and community.

LYOTARD'S INTERPRETATION OF KANT

Lyotard develops an interpretation of Kant in *L'Enthousiasme: la critique kantienne de l'histoire* (1986) and *Leçons sur l'analytique du sublime* (1991). These books incorporate well-known essays on Kant in a modified form, notably, 'Introduction à une étude du politique selon Kant' and 'L'archipel et le signe (sur la pensée kantienne de l'historico-politique)' in the former, and 'L'intérêt du sublime' and, to some extent, 'Sensus communis' for the latter. These works overlap to a very great extent and can be divided into essays that prepare for or explain Lyotard's use of Kant for the benefit of his own philosophy and the book that actually delivers that philosophy (*The Differend*). For example, with the exception of chapters IV and V, *L'Enthousiasme* is almost a verbatim repetition of work done in *The Differend*. Similarly, most of the lecture notes collected in *Leçons sur l'analytique du sublime* are expressed in a much tighter form in *The Differend*. The publication dates of these texts are therefore misleading and it would be wrong to think that the two later works add to the earlier one. That continuation and application of the politics of the differend takes place in *L'Inhumain* and *Moralités postmodernes*; they will be studied here in Chapter 6.

Put simply, Lyotard's interpretation involves a deepening of the gulf that Kant deduces between the realms of pure reason and practical reason. This gulf is described at length in the introduction to Kant's *Critique of Judgement*. It is a gulf between the realm of the natural concept of the understanding that must be in conformity with the law of causality and the realm of the concept of freedom that must be in conformity with the categorical imperative. The first realm is the sensible, that is, phenomena or intuitions that can be presented to confirm or deny a concept of the understanding. The second realm is the supersensible, that is, the realm of things in themselves that cannot be intuited. Thus, we know that a scientific concept must be in conformity with the law of causality and that we can confirm a concept by presenting a phenomenon, constituted by the transcendental subject, that accords with it. But a moral law, which we select to guide our free actions, must be consistent with the categorical imperative and we cannot give evidence for it since it has no objective reality. So what the gulf implies is that we cannot legitimately apply causality to moral laws nor subject them to demands of evidence. It also means that we cannot legitimately assume that freedom exists in the realm of the sensible, nor seek to confirm moral laws as laws of nature, that is, of the sensible realm.

Why is this gulf problematic? The answer comes from the set of impossibilities outlined above. Two distinct and important aspects of reason have to be kept apart in a way that is detrimental to both. We cannot appeal to science and to laws of nature in questions of morality. We cannot confirm moral acts in nature. But moral acts, our free adoption of moral laws, are meant to bring about a more just and harmonious nature, at least to the degree that we are part of it: 'the concept of freedom is meant to actualise in the sensible world the end proposed by its laws; and nature must consequently also be capable of being regarded in such a way that in conformity to law of its form it at least harmonises with the possibility of the ends to be effectuated in it according to the laws of freedom' (Kant 1980: 14). So, over and above the fact that humans must be awkwardly thought of as causally determined *qua* natural phenomena and free *qua* moral agents, their actions as moral agents become closed in on themselves, in the sense of being incapable of confirmation. In the context of Lyotard's concerns with regard to nihilism, this incapacity is troublesome since it obliges us to act for the better with no possible evidence that our acts have or indeed can achieve it. It would be wrong, though, to assume that this is Lyotard's original angle on Kant. Lyotard's work on the faculties is fairly orthodox and the critique of the gulf between the faculties stretches back to Hegel. Indeed, Kant is in many ways in advance of this critique and careful to exploit the gulf between the faculties as an opportunity, since it preserves a moral realm free from the demands of causality. Lyotard's original work on Kant is in his use of the feeling of the sublime in the context of the possibility of common aesthetic and, hence, political senses.

For Kant, it is possible to bridge the gulf between nature and freedom, but only in one direction and with restrictions:

> The concept of freedom determines nothing in respect of the theoretical cognition of nature; and the concept of nature likewise nothing in respect of the practical laws of freedom. To that extent, then, it is not possible to throw a bridge from the one realm to the other. – Yet although the determining grounds of causality according to the concept of freedom (and the practical rules that this contains) have no place in nature, and the sensible cannot determine the supersensible in the Subject; still the converse is possible (not, it is true, in respect of the knowledge of nature, but of the consequences arising from the supersensible and bearing on the sensible).

> (Kant 1980: 37)

So it is conceded that theoretical reason has no priority over practical reason, science has no priority over morality. But practical reason can determine the realm of pure reason, not in terms of what can be known, for this still has to be in conformity with causality, but in terms of 'the consequences arising from the supersensible and bearing on the sensible'. Kant argues that it is possible to *judge* – not to know – that a free act is confirmed in nature. Thus the confirmation that seemed to be missing in terms of our free acts as moral agents is available – not in terms of cause, but in terms of judgements concerning ends.

Thus we cannot say 'this practical act caused this natural phenomenon', but we can say 'this natural phenomenon appears to have this end or purpose', where the end or purpose is practical in the sense of being the result of freedom (it would make no sense to speak of ends or purposes where there was only causal determination). The latter statement allows for judgements concerning the unity of nature and morality: this or that purpose in the realm of freedom (moral laws) must be possible in terms of judgements concerning the purpose or end of natural phenomena: 'The effect in accordance with the concept of freedom is the final end which (or the manifestation of which in the sensible world) is to exist, and this presupposes the condition of the possibility of that end in nature (i.e. in the nature of the Subject as a being of the sensible world, namely, as man)' (Kant 1980: 37–8). So although science cannot determine free acts, our knowledge of nature determines what free acts are possible and confirms the ends implied by those acts. For example, let a set of freely adopted laws have the purpose of a harmonious human society. This purpose is limited by our knowledge of humans as part of nature and possibly confirmed by our judgements concerning the purpose of nature. Here at least the gulf between nature and moral laws is bridged: '[The faculty of judgement] with its concept of a finality of nature, provides us with the mediating concept between concepts of nature and the concept of freedom – a concept that makes possible the transition from the pure theoretical [legislation of the understanding] to the pure practical [legislation of reason] and from conformity to law in accordance with the former to final ends according to the latter' (38).

This bridge is essential to the Kantian project in allowing it to develop and flourish as a philosophy that unifies knowledge, morality and our capacity to make judgements concerning ends. It becomes capable of putting forward a critical study of the relations that hold between nature (the realm of understanding), art (the realm of judgement) and freedom (the realm of practical reason). Art is the realm of judgement because judgement applies to our faculty to feel (pleasure and pain), rather than to know (understand) or to desire (rationally choose to act according to a given moral law). Kant's critical philosophy breaks out from a rather sterile deduction of impassable gulfs into a more productive critical discussion of what bridging judgements are legitimate and what conclusions can be drawn from them. For example, in his *Kant's Aesthetic Theory* (1997), Salim Kemal notes how teleological judgement, that is, judgement concerning ends, makes natural beauty and fine art possible. Without the validity of these judgements we could not speak of nature except in terms of causes, and certainly not in terms of the pleasure or purpose associated with natural beauty: '[teleological judgement] allows us to see objects as art – as the product of ratiocinative human willing rather than as the effect of determinate causes – and thence as fine art when these judgements satisfy our judgements of taste' (159).

Politics and culture as instruments of human community can legitimately enter Kantian philosophy at this point. They do not do so in terms of specific final political and aesthetic judgements taken to be valid for all members of the community ('This is the beautiful'; 'This is progress'), but as the faculty that allows for discussions concerning, say, the beautiful and political progress ('The proper framework for discussion concerning art and politics is provided by judgements concerning ends and the evidence we may have for the validity of those judgements'). This sense of community is the point where Lyotard's and Kant's projects seem furthest apart. The former develops a philosophy of radical differences that separate communities around conflicts called differends; he then defines the task of a certain philosophy and politics as bearing witness to differends. The latter allows for the definition of a global aesthetic and political community; the task of philosophy here is to remind us that it is not a community of fixed values, but one of a commitment to rational deliberation about judgements of value. This dual concern forms one of the Kantian definitions of *sensus communis* as a critical faculty allowing for that rational commitment.

According to Kant, in the *Critique of Judgement*, *sensus communis* is then an openness to differences about values guided by a commitment to the development of common judgement:

> by the name *sensus communis* is to be understood the idea of a *public* sense, i.e. a critical faculty which in its reflective act takes account (*a priori*) of the mode of representation of everyone else, in order, *as it were*, to weigh its judgement with the collective reason of mankind, and thereby avoid the illusion arising from subjective and personal conditions which could readily be taken for objective, an illusion that would exert a prejudicial influence upon its judgement.
>
> (Kant 1980: 151)

So with *sensus communis* Kant wants to avoid the trap of making general statements on the basis of subjective views. But he is also constructing a space for collective judgements based on a balancing out of subjective judgements with a reflection on the judgements of others. This reading of *sensus communis* places Kant at the very heart of a modern critical enlightenment, working towards a differentiated and reflexively critical community: 'Given the substantive notion of universality that seems to be at work in Kant's sensus communis, our search for community and universality does not lead to homogeneity. We recognise differences between ourselves as well

105

as those features of our subjectivity which we share with and which are compatible with others' subjectivity' (Kemal 1997: 163).

This conclusion is of grave concern to Lyotard. He often returns to the passage quoted above at key moments in his works on Kant (*Leçons sur l'analytique du sublime*: 262–7; *The Differend*: 241; 'Sensus communis': *passim*). The general line of his argument is that there is a possible confusion between a transcendental and an anthropological interpretation of *sensus communis*. This line is also pursued in Lyotard's essay on Hannah Arendt, 'Survivant: Arendt' in *Lectures d'enfance* (1991c): 'I repeat, here, that Arendt's views on the shareability of sensus communis are won at the expense of an abusively sociologising reading of the Kantian "sensus communis". Certainly, his text lends itself to this because anthropology is not eliminated from it, as would have been required by the transcendental analysis' (86). I have not studied this later political essay in depth due to its strong relations to Lyotard's work on Kant and the sublime and other later essays considered in Chapter 6. It is, however, an important political essay on Arendt.

Broadly, *sensus communis* can either be taken as a supersensible sense that we all share by transcendental necessity or as a necessary empirical procedure for developing a community while taking account of differences in matters of art and morality. In both cases, *sensus communis* is identified very strongly with the Kantian deduction of the necessity of sharing the capacity to make judgements of taste ('*Taste* is the faculty of estimating an object or a mode of representation by means of a delight or aversion *apart from any interest*. The object of such a delight is called *beautiful*' (Kant 1980: 50)). Kant deduces this necessity by appealing to universal subjective conditions that make it necessary for us to be able to make judgements of taste: 'This pleasure must of necessity depend for every one upon the same conditions, seeing that they are the subjective conditions of the possibility of a cognition in general, and the proportion of these cognitive faculties which is requisite for taste is requisite also for ordinary sound understanding, the presence of which we are entitled to presuppose in everyone' (150). Judgements of taste involve the harmonious use of the understanding, reason and aesthetic judgement in recognising cognitive and moral disinterestedness allied to pleasure.

Lyotard has no problem with the sharing of a necessary capacity to make such judgements; in fact, his whole approach to Kant's text is to attempt to define *sensus communis* as the transcendental condition for a shared taste and thence to restrict this universal sense to the beautiful. In so doing, he keeps the sense within the boundaries of a very specific type of aesthetic appreciation ('We all share the possibility of making judgements concerning the beautiful defined as "interest without interest"'). *Sensus communis* is, then, not a bridge between faculties as a mode of judgement that allows for a general sense of community to emerge in morality, politics, aesthetics.

It is merely a necessary condition for making judgements concerning the beautiful that involves a supersensible and harmonious employment of understanding, judgement and reason: 'The possibility of sharing is a transcendental character of taste. It requires in turn a transcendental supplement, the Idea of the supersensible' (*Leçons sur l'analytique du sublime*: 262). The insistence on the role of the supersensible is important here since it seems to debar *sensus communis* from any involvement with actual judgements concerning objects and to restrict it to the subjective. It is therefore not a bridge between different realms and it certainly cannot allow us to 'recognise differences' in order to build a sense of community, since it quite specifically does not allow for judgements concerning actual differences of taste.

However, a second way of defining *sensus communis*, whilst still starting from Kant's deduction of the necessity of sharing taste, takes the definition of the *sensus* as supersensible a step further by claiming that it is not only the harmonious employment of the faculties that is necessarily shared, but also the communicability of judgements dependent on that employment. This move is essential if we want to be able to say that we do not only share the capacity to make judgements of taste, but that we necessarily share a way to arrive at shared actual judgements of taste. This way would be *sensus communis* as described in the passage quoted above from section 40 of the *Critique of Judgement*. It is defended by Kemal in his interpretation of the *Critique of Judgement*: 'Kant's move [to a discussion concerning actual judgements] suggests that he distinguishes between two kinds of necessity, and finds in sensus communis the criteria for success in actual judgements' (Kemal 1997: 67). This statement is itself controversial in Kantian studies. For different reasons, commentators other than Lyotard refuse to allow or give a different explanation for this move into the actual (see, for example, Guyer, *Kant and the Claims of Taste* (1997) and Makkreel, *Imagination and Interpretation in Kant: the Hermeneutical Import of the Critique of Judgement* (1990)).

Lyotard sides with the more sceptical position concerning actual judgements of taste because of a strong opposition to the requirement to take into account the 'mode of representation of anyone else': 'The delicate point is the anyone else' (*Leçons sur l'analytique du sublime*: 263). If this is taken to mean that it is necessary and possible to take someone else's view into account in forming a *sensus communis*, then it cancels his attempts to define the differend as an unbridgeable conflict. His politics of resistance to hegemony (including hegemony achieved through the means most respectful of differences) would founder on this possible communication. So he proposes a counter-interpretation of the key passage. It is not to be taken literally as an appeal to a capacity to reflect on a position other than one's own, but as an explanation of how '*a power of appreciation*' takes into consideration, '*Rücksicht nimmt*', another, '*anderen*' whatever it may be, '*jedes*' (262). This is not a mere scholastic point or battle of translations. Lyotard wants to insist that the reflection of the *sensus communis* is internal to a thought process that, in presupposing communicability, presupposes other possible tastes.

There is therefore no need and no legitimacy in passing over to an actual encounter with another: 'The aesthetic "community" is not constituted first by the opinions given by individuals. It "unfolds" so to speak thanks to a work of variations that "thought" and thought alone, in "Gedanken", puts into effect in order to escape from its "private" condition. Deprived of the other by its own act of appreciation' (264). The harmony between faculties implied by taste and the beautiful remains only a transcendental condition. It does not become a basis for an actual politics based around the *sensus communis* defined as a procedure. But this is only one leg of Lyotard's relation to Kant. He also wants to deduce the opposite to this procedure, this time not around the beautiful, but around the sublime. The point will be to show that the condition for the feeling of the sublime is the disharmony of faculties and the disturbance of the *sensus* to deduce the opposite of this procedure: 'Neither moral universality, nor aesthetic universalisation, but instead the destruction of one by the other through the violence of their differend that is the sublime. The differend itself cannot insist on being shared by any thought, even when considered subjectively' (286). A two-fold politics is suggested in these last lines of *Leçons sur l'analytique du sublime*. There is an appeal to the sublime against community, defined either as moral universality or as the use of aesthetics to achieve a political teleology directed towards universality. There is also an appeal against any conception of subjective unity. These come together in the crucial politics of the differend outlined in the latter chapters of *The Differend*.

Prior to the study of this politics we can now answer the questions raised with Jean-Loup Thébaud above.

1   On the relation of 'judgement without criteria' to knowledge. Lyotard exploits the radical nature of his interpretation of the gulf between faculties to eliminate knowledge from politics and ethics. Politics is a struggle over realms that can have no final determinant rule as to which claims are true or good, whereas ethics is the realm governed by an absolute obligation to the other. So, in the former, knowledge claims are but one type of political move. In the latter, it is illegitimate to claim to know the other. The relation between moral and political judgement and knowledge is one of incommensurability. Cognitive statements (phrases, in the terminology of the differend) have no legitimacy in the fields of morality or politics and vice versa, because the laws that apply legitimately to the field of knowledge are incommensurable with the laws of the other fields. With Kant, this is a matter of causality and freedom. In *The Differend*, Lyotard translates this as

an incommensurability of the stakes that govern an appropriate concatenation of phrases within a genre, for example: 'The stakes implied in the tragic genre, its intended success (shall we say the feelings of fear and pity on the part of its addressees) and the stakes implied in the technical genre, its own success (shall we say the availability of the referent for the addressor's wants) are for their part incommensurable . . .' (TD: 128). Scientific and ethical claims cannot legitimately resolve political conflicts because, for Lyotard, politics is the 'lawless' struggle between realms or faculties. The worst conflicts arise, at least with regard to the differend, when politics is taken as a genre and given an illusory stake: 'Politics always gives rise to misunderstandings because it takes place as a genre' (141). So the political, with respect to Lyotard's philosophy of the differend, is to further the awareness that there are no finally legitimate stakes in politics: 'At the same time, though, politics is not at all a genre, it bears witness to the nothingness which opens up with each occurring phrase and on the occasion of which the differend between genres of discourse is born' (141). It is in this sense that the political is judgement without criteria. It is an intervention in politics, in the name of differends, that must remind us of the impossibility of final just judgements, but without depending on them: 'One's responsibility before thought consists . . . in detecting differends and in finding the (impossible) idiom for phrasing them.'

2 In terms of Thébaud's questions concerning the existence of laws in ethics, Lyotard agrees that there are such laws – although the number and extent of them are minimal. However, the full force of Thébaud's questions lies in the possibility of extending these ethical laws into the political realm, that is, to give the ethical a determinant role in politics. But this cannot take place for the reasons outlined in the previous point. So, it is true that judgement in ethics has criteria to follow and these may be formed in accordance with the Kantian Categorical Imperative or, for Lyotard, according to Levinas's rule 'that the you is never the I, and that the I is never the you' (114). But, in both cases, these criteria have no legitimacy outside their proper field (moral laws). We are not justified in applying moral laws to nature or to any other field (genre) whose stakes are incommensurable with the ethical genre of obligation to a primary principle – Kantian or Levinasian.

3 Finally, in response to questions regarding the presupposition of a political community by politics, Lyotard points out that no given community, defined by science, morality or ethics, can lay claim to be that community. This is because his idea of politics as struggle presupposes differends rather than any form of homogeneity. If there is a presupposed political community, it can be defined on the grounds of neither knowledge nor ethics. There is no natural or ethical community because a political community emerges exactly when we have to bring the ethical, the natural

and the aesthetic together. Any rule that guides the formation of this community must bridge between these incommensurable fields. This bridging cannot take place legitimately but only 'as if' it is legitimate: 'Causality through freedom gives signs, never ascertainable effects, nor chains of effects. No "nature", not even a supersensible one, not even as an Idea, can result from obligation. The imperative does not command one to act so as to produce a community of practical reasonable beings, but as if the maxim of action were supposed to be a maxim of this community' (127). In addition to this turn away from an ethical community, the range of traditional ways of defining a legitimate politics is rejected by Lyotard on the grounds that it is anthropological and thus an illegitimate extension of the realm of knowledge: 'The terms democracy, autocracy, oligarchy, monarchy, and anarchy (which designate modes of government) and those of republic and despotism (which designate modes of domination or authorization) belong to narrowly anthropological or politico-logical descriptions' (142).

In many ways, though, these answers only succeed in so far as they raise new questions concerning the ways in which 'we' come to feel the differend and become aware of the gulf between faculties or the incommensurability of genres. By *The Differend*, Lyotard is much more clear as to why a form of 'judgement without criteria' is important in terms of the political, but he is less clear on how the testimony for differends or irresolvable conflicts can constitute such a judgement and, indeed, overcome its implicit paradoxes. The answers also raise questions concerning the relation of Lyotard's politics of the differend to traditional, and by his own admission, necessary forms of politics ('What politics is about and what distinguishes various kinds of politics is the genre of discourse, or the stakes, whereby differends are formulated as litigations and find their "regulation"' (142)). The sections that follow put forward a critical interpretation of Lyotard's communication of the differend through the feeling of the sublime and his justification of the role played by the differend in the political. The next chapter explains and criticises his development of that role in the essays published after *The Differend*.

JUSTIFYING THE DIFFEREND

What does this 'as if' mean for Lyotard? His interpretation of Kant departs from the norm in not taking transcendental deductions as the crux of Kantian argument. Instead, while recognising the importance of the deductions, Lyotard does not take them as the final arbiters of Kantian philosophy, where the success or failure of the latter is inextricably linked to the validity of the former. Instead, he reads Kant's text as itself driven more by a manner or art of reflexive thinking than by a method of transcendental deductions: 'But, in my opinion aesthetic judgement conceals a more important secret than the one of doctrine. It is the secret of the "manner" (rather than the method) by which critical thought proceeds in general' (*Leçons sur l'analytique du sublime*: 19).

According to Lyotard, Kant's critical philosophy is developed thanks to a 'feel for the unity in a presentation' that must be present prior to any transcendental deduction: 'Now, by definition, the mode of critical thought could not be purely reflexive (it does not already have the concepts whose usage it seeks to establish). What is more, aesthetic judgement manifests reflection in its most "autonomous" state, the most naked, if you will' (20). This interpretation is consistent with Kant's later texts, notably 'What is orientation in thinking?', where Kant argues for the unity of the faculties in reason as a 'need': 'It is at this point, however, that the right of the need of reason supervenes as a subjective ground for presupposing and accepting something which reason cannot presume to know on objective grounds, and hence for orienting ourselves in thought . . .' (240–41). The need for unity is the sign that gives a well-determined direction to thought. It allows us to follow a specific line even before there are any critical justifications for taking that line. But, more than that, it also allows us to proceed where critical thought cannot of right – with the proviso, though, that this process is itself limited by critique as to the claims it may make. In 'What is orientation in thinking?', this is the main point of Kant's argument. He wants to allow for reason to proceed against the strong claims of scepticism (that can even come out of *Critique*, 246), but without falling back on to pre-critical dogma.

It is on the nature of this pre-critical need that Lyotard again departs from a reading of Kant that allows for reason to proceed in a sure-footed manner across divides between faculties. As in his treatment of *sensus communis*, Lyotard argues that this need is either purely supersensible and hence of no use in the justification of a bridge between the sensible and the supersensible, or it is an anthropological observation and hence devoid of any universalisability. The need of reason cannot justify Kant's claims and involves him in a viciously circular argument:

It remains that if the critical watchman thinks he can supplement for the absence of a legal provision and go ahead and pass sentence over the differend concerning freedom it is because he believes himself to be authorized by the Idea that nature pursues its end by means of this supplementarity . . . Since it's an Idea (that of nature and thus of ends), he cannot present an ostensible this to validate the authorization. He can present an 'as-if-this,' an analogon, a sign. That sign is his feeling, the feeling that one ought to and is able to judge even in the absence of laws. This feeling, however, is in turn only a proof (*Beweisen*) certifying that there is a right and a duty to judge outside the law if some nature pursues its ends by means of this feeling. No exit is made from this circle.

(TD: 135)

However, the point of Lyotard's interpretation is not simply to remain in the position of hopeless and dangerous scepticism feared by Kant in 'What is orientation in thinking?' ('the way is wide open for every kind of zealotry, superstition and even atheism' (246)). Instead, he is interested in the way pre-critical thinking and post-critical bridging necessarily involve an accommodation with feelings as signs: 'if the third *Critique* can fulfil its mission of unifying the philosophical field, it is above all not because its theme exposes the regulative Idea of an objective finality of nature, it is because it makes manifest, under the banner of aesthetics, the reflexive manner of thinking that is at work in all of the critical texts' (*Leçons sur l'analytique du sublime*: 21). So Lyotard gives priority to feelings and to the limitations and impulses they give to thought, as opposed to the regulative role of Ideas. We feel; the feeling compels us to think and to think in a certain way. Does this allow us to bridge between faculties, albeit in a manner independent of a necessary law?

The answer lies in reflexive judgement by analogy. This reflexive manner is to think by applying models that are legitimate in a given realm 'as if' they are also legitimate in others, where this thought is itself a response to a feeling that unites two realms. The feeling is a sign that we may suppose that the laws from one realm are valid in another. The sign works because it is at the same time a testimony to the heterogeneity of the realms and to our subjective compulsion to unite them. The only way to resolve this apparent tension is to judge that the realms can be united, but to give no objective validity to that judgement: to judge 'as if' the unity is possible. Lyotard's most clear treatment of this can be found in *L'Enthousiasme*, where the possibility of a Kantian politics and history is considered on the basis of a reading of Kant's late political essays. In the book, Lyotard makes his claim more precise by stating that we may pass from one realm to another by applying 'the form' of laws from one realm to another. Thus we do not suppose that given laws are valid across realms, but that the principles that govern their formation hold in both. This formal correspondence is what he means by judgement by analogy. For example, we treat nature as if it conforms to finality in response to the feeling of pleasure that occurs with natural beauty. Similar arguments are developed between the realm of judgement and the realm of freedom, where we take the beautiful as the symbol for (as if it were) the morally good. Each time the use of the 'as if' indicates an operation of aesthetic judgement in a non-necessary fashion, a speculative bridging (31–44).

However, at all times, these passages are subject to the circle described above; we may feel obliged to think in this way or that, but we cannot ultimately justify doing so. The universal claims of Kant's politics founder at this point as they become contingent on a shared feeling. In *L'Enthousiasme* and to a lesser extent in *The Differend*, Lyotard is prepared to admit that many of Kant's political feelings were so widespread as to appear universal. But he wants to insist that this consensus has broken down in contemporary politics. The events and feelings that mark our time indicate an abyss between faculties, genres and hence political positions. There is still some sense of community in these feelings, but it is a contrary one. It is common sense that there can be no community beyond that sense – though this is correct only if we remember that in *L'Enthousiasme* Lyotard is using 'common sense' in a meaning doubly removed from everyday usage: 'The occasions given to this highly developed "sense of community" would be called: Auschwitz, an abyss that opens when we have present an object capable of validating the phrase of the Idea of human rights; Budapest 1956, an abyss that opens before the Idea of the right of a people . . .' (108). The task of a just contemporary politics, defined first only by its feelings, is to bear witness to these abysses, that is, to bear witness to the differend. But is not this use of 'just' in conjunction with 'contemporary' as illegitimate as Kant's?

Lyotard's philosophy of the differend needs more than mere observation. It must establish that we cannot bridge between realms or genres of discourse, if it is to live up to its claims to a higher justice: 'By showing that the linking of one phrase onto another is problematic and that this problem is the problem of politics, to set up a philosophical politics apart from the politics of intellectuals and of politicians' (TD: xiii). But has not this already been shown in Lyotard's sceptical reading of Kant? That is, if we take the transcendental deductions as the final word on legitimacy over given realms, then the impossibility of bridging has been set up and needs no further work. Yet that only allows for critique, as a transcendental ruling over what can and what cannot be said legitimately. The politics of the differend requires actual specificity. Lyotard needs to be able to say in specific cases 'this is a sign of a gulf or a differend'. This is not the same as saying 'this statement that bridges between two realms is necessarily illegitimate'. Indeed, the former appears to rule out the latter; a gulf or a differend is not a matter of signs of actual cases, but a transcendental matter, a condition of the possibility of legitimate rules in given realms. Yet he insists on the possibility of feeling specific differends, rather than deducing their abstract necessity.

The argument for this occurs in his reading of the section 'A renewed attempt to answer the question: "Is the human race continually improving?"' from Kant's last large work, *The Contest of Faculties*, reproduced in *Political Writings* (1990). The problem of the gulf separating causal nature and the realm of freedom is stated crudely at paragraph 4 of the section: 'For we are dealing with freely acting beings to whom one can *dictate* in advance what they *ought* to do, but of whom one cannot *predict* what they actually *will* do . . .' (180). So it appears that we cannot predict improvement because any evidence as to objective human behaviour can always be contradicted by human freedom, since the former does not have a causal relation with the latter. In the necessary absence of objective evidence for improvement, Kant turns to the possibility of a subjective 'quality or power of being the cause' of improvement confirmed by objective evidence: 'In human affairs, there must be some experience or other which, as an event which has actually occurred, might suggest that man has the quality or power of being the cause and (since his actions are supposed to be those of a being endowed with freedom) the author of his own improvement' (181).

At first, there appears to be no reason to give any credence whatsoever to this move. It appears merely to establish an obscure but nonetheless illegitimate causal chain from nature to freedom and from freedom to nature (event as evidence for supersensible capacity; supersensible capacity as evidence for objective improvement). But this is exactly what interests Lyotard. Kant seeks to break the causal chain by making the first evidence merely 'indicate' the power and the power merely to be a 'historical sign' of improvement. This is thinking 'as if' the realms can meet. As such, it would appear to fall foul of the analysis given above. But, according to Lyotard, this need not be the case.

Unlike a judgement by analogy, the thought process instantiated by the feeling of the sublime is a negative one, specifically, 'it is impossible to confirm this Idea that bridges between two realms or two sides of a differend'. The impossibility is the result of the conjunction of pleasure taken in attempting to furnish such evidence with the pain of its failure. Of importance for Lyotard's argument (developed in the 'Notice Kant 4' section of *The Differend*: 161–71) is that the negative thought is based on the feeling of the sublime associated with a given failure to present. For example, in attempting to gauge the size of a sublime 'object', to present the object as having this or that great size, we cannot bring an intuition in accord with a concept. Our sensible experience of, say, a mountain or massive construction is not determined and stable enough to connect with a properly formed concept of the understanding. So, even though the exemplary enormity or greatness of the thing should allow us to come to terms with great size or grandeur, that task proves beyond the faculties that should be up to it. Similarly, in attempting to gauge the political significance of the acts involved in the French revolution, spectators cannot make these accord with an Idea of reason such as that humans are capable of progress. We have an Idea of humanity in progress but when we attempt to make that coincide with the acts, we fail.

The Kantian definition of an Idea of reason is that it is an idea, derived from a concept of the understanding, for which it is impossible to present an intuition. Thus, from the concept 'human', we derive the Idea of humanity though we cannot offer an intuition for that Idea. In the formulation of Ideas of reason, we start with a concept and, quite legitimately and necessarily, given the demand for completion in reason, logically expand it by moving, for example, from great to greatest or from part to whole. Though it is a requirement for the concept to be in conformity with an intuition, this cannot be the case for the idea, given a limitation on the faculty of imagination; it is not capable of representing the greatest size or the whole of humanity. Kant's discussion of ideas in the *Critique of Pure Reason* (314) explains to some extent why Lyotard insists on using Ideas with a capital (as I have done here) since it is easy to fall into confusion concerning the right sense of the term – as it is now even more common to call an intuition an idea (as in: 'my idea of the colour red') than when Kant was writing. Lyotard's use of the term is built upon an interpretation of section 27 of the *Critique of Judgement*:

> The feeling of the sublime is, therefore, at once a feeling of dis-
> pleasure, arising from the inadequacy of imagination in the aesthetic
> estimation of magnitude to attain to its estimation by reason, and a
> simultaneous awakened pleasure, arising from this very judgement
> of the inadequacy of the greatest faculty of sense being in accord
> with ideas of reason, so far as the effort to attain these is for us a law.
>
> (106)

There is pain in the necessary failure of the imagination in the task of presenting an intuition that conforms with an Idea of reason. But this does not simply turn us away from such attempts, because there is also pleasure in the realisation that it is necessary for us to seek to offer such intuitions: 'Enthusiasm is a modality of the feeling of the sublime. The imagination tries to supply a direct, sensible presentation for an Idea of reason . . . It does not succeed and it thereby feels its impotence, but at the same time it discovers its destination, which is to bring itself into harmony with the Ideas of reason, through an appropriate presentation' (*The Differend*: 165). The conjunction of pleasure and pain in the sublime overcomes the paradox of a search for something impossible, at least in the sense where we are left with a continuing drive to further the demand that nature be brought into accord with reason. So if the feeling of the sublime is widespread in the presence of a particular event, then it is also a sign of a potential for progress in the human race, since we share a faculty that drives us to act in a positive way with respect to differends or to the gulf between realms. This is why Kant's case in 'Is the human race continually improving?' is proven, at least according to Lyotard's interpretation.

Notwithstanding the tendentiousness of his interpretation, given its dependence on a very narrow view of the Kantian sublime and on an insertion of that view into a text that does not overtly call for it, Lyotard has at least provided an argument for the case. But his point is doubly difficult. First, it does not quite do what Kant sets out to achieve since the particularity of the sublime sign is to leave the spectator in a confused state, caught between action and inaction or success and failure: 'the "passage" does not quite take place, it is a "passage" in the course of coming to pass. Its course, its movement, is a kind of agitation on the spot, one within the impasse of incommensurability, and above the abyss, a "vibration," as Kant writes, that is, "a quickly alternating attraction toward, and repulsion from, the same object" (*Critique of Judgement*, § 27). Such is the state of Gemüt for the spectators of the French revolution' (*The Differend*: 167). So the sublime is not a sign that the human race is improving in the strong Kantian enlightenment sense of acting positively on a feeling that drives us to change the world according to reason: 'They will thereby enter into a constitution based on genuine principles of right, which is by its very nature capable of constant progress and improvement without forfeiting its strength' (Kant 1990: 189).

According to Lyotard, rights, constitutions and progress towards a rational unity cannot be driven by the sublime. If the feeling allows for an orientation in politics, it is a negative one of limits and barriers. This has its positive side, as a drive to testify to differences against illegitimate attempts to bridge them. But even this has a serious and ultimately damning flaw. The second difficulty in Lyotard's argument is that it falls foul of his own critique of Kant. The sublime may well indicate an inability to pass judgement across a divide, but that is in no way an argument for the claim that it is always impossible to pass such a judgement. Lyotard's later work is, in fact, more dependent on anthropology than Kant's. He cannot show that what the feeling indicates is in any way necessary. He cannot even show that the feeling has any lasting effect on a given spectator; that it has occurred once in a given situation is no guarantee that it will occur again. Given these singular failures, it is important to ask what becomes of the politics of testifying to the differend announced at the beginning of *The Differend*.

THE POLITICS OF THE DIFFEREND

The political aim of testifying to the differend has a strong attraction so long as we accept that the differences involved genuinely cannot be bridged. But, because Lyotard's philosophy depends on the contingency of particular feelings of the sublime, he is never in a position to prove that any given difference is absolute. He can say 'At this moment my feelings stop me from attempting to bridge this difference with the aid of this Idea of reason'. But in no way does this amount to proving that, say, the Idea of humanity is never capable of resolving a difference. He is not even in the position of saying that the idea will not serve for others or even for himself once the feeling of the sublime subsides.

It often seems that his philosophy of language and his view of genres and specific differends leads to the political aim of giving voice to one or other oppressed side of a differend. But, given the necessity of his resort to the feeling of the sublime in his crucial encounter with Kant, that kind of testimony is limited in how it can be given and in what it can achieve. It is not the case that by simply giving voice to a victim of terror, one testifies to the differend. That expression must at least aim to cause a feeling of the sublime in the spectator. This is not the case in most instances. For example, modern enlightened media have taken on the tasks of uncovering injustice and of seeking to mobilise their readers, viewers and listeners. That mobilisation is very rarely based on the limiting and vainly agitated feeling of the sublime, indeed, this would be an effect that ran counter to the progressive aims of some sections of a modern media.

So Lyotard cannot simply advocate a politics of uncovering and expression. The way in which these take place must present an Idea of reason and, at the same time, show that it cannot be validated while paradoxically validating it as something that attracts us and forces us into action. A sublime event must be presented to achieve that validation. This object could never be simply one side of a differend. On the contrary, it has to be an object that conjures up and dashes the attempt to bring both sides together. But this also implies that we cannot do justice to the terrorised side except by subsuming its claims under the more general notion of doing justice to the possibility of incommensurability and the differend against Ideas of reason. There is a detached hardness to this politics: 'Your plight calls the spectator to the differend.' There is also a nihilistic fatalism: 'And this general differend can never be resolved.' In the next chapter, I will study some of the most important essays written by Lyotard after *The Differend* in order to show how they are applications of this political and philosophical method and how they exhibit this harshness and nihilism, despite other merits.

A negative critical conclusion must be arrived at after this study of the role of judgement in Lyotard's philosophy of the differend. I shall put this critique in terms of the questions about judgement that remain unanswered from the first section of this chapter:

4 The highest form of judgement cannot be claimed for political and philosophical judgements concerning differends. These judgements are restricted to singular instants where there is a feeling of the sublime and are closed to any outside inspection or even retrospection. There cannot therefore be a sense of highest operating between forms of judgement. However, Lyotard is justified in defending that closure; there may be a form

of judgement based on the sublime that does not allow for assessment independent of its own criterion (that a feeling of the sublime is felt).

5   The politics of the differend is not viable in terms of reliability; that is, it cannot guarantee that its judgements will last any longer than a given 'experience' of the feeling of the sublime. Neither is it viable in terms of general conceptions of judgement; that is, its claims to justice cannot be inspected. So, not only is it a politics that testifies to absolute differences; it also depends illegitimately on an agreement with that notion of difference for its own claims to justice if those claims are given any validity beyond a given experience of the feeling of the sublime.

6   Due to its dependence on unpredictable occurrences of the feeling of the sublime, the politics of the differend cannot be well defined in terms of what it stands for, including absolute difference. Instead, it acquires a minimal consistency from the internal logic of that feeling; that is, the politics of the differend depends upon but is also defined by the triggering of a simultaneous attraction to and failure of an Idea of reason.

6

THE SUBLIME AND POLITICS

THE DIFFEREND AND POLITICAL PRAGMATICS

After the work on Kant and judgement in *The Differend*, Lyotard's philosophy is directed to a sophisticated political pragmatics. This is driven by the problem of how to testify to the differend, given the restriction imposed on the testimony by the relation that holds between the feeling of the sublime and Ideas of reason (such as 'Humanity is progressing'). The only way to testify is to conjure up an Idea and to dash the possibility of presenting it in an actual case. So Lyotard's work becomes practical in two ways. First, there is the selection of an Idea and a particular case apt to show its failure. Second, there is a selection of the right way to instil a feeling of the sublime, that is, both an attraction to the possibility of an actual presentation of the Idea and an aversion to the actual presentation in a given case. These practical considerations are companions to the argument I put forward in the conclusion to the previous chapter; that is, that Lyotard can never testify directly to a given differend, to a given absolute difference. His testimony must always pass through an Idea; the feelings instilled in the addressees are not directed to the actual conflict but to the necessity and failure of the Idea in actuality. The testimony to the differend disappears as a direct engagement with an irresolvable difference and moves towards an undermining of that which would resolve such differences.

Perhaps the most striking aspect of this pragmatics is its negativity. The particular is tackled through the medium of a universal in a way that negates the desire to treat each particular case for itself. The universal is taken on with a view to bind it to the feeling of the sublime in order to show the limitations of the Idea. The feeling of the sublime puts the addressee into a disabling tension that negates pleasure with pain and vice versa. There is no escaping this, since it is the result of Lyotard's arguments concerning Kant's deduction of the gulf between faculties. These are essential for Lyotard's deduction of the possibility of the differend and of the incommensurability of genres. However much it offends feelings for direct positive action, the political, as thought through the differend, can only be resistance to the hegemony of Ideas of reason in particular cases. In the last section of this chapter, I will consider the question of whether this definition of resistance still allows for a positive creative attitude to matter as defined by Lyotard in his later essays *L'Inhumain* (1988c) and *Moralités postmodernes* (1993b).

From the point of view of Lyotard's libidinal politics, the dependence on negation is nihilistic. The objection does not lie in the feeling of the sublime as such, but in the practical aim to seek out that desire because of its effect on our relation to Ideas of reason. The principal desire in the politics of the differend is a negative one: to negate Ideas of reason as ways of bridging differends. What is more, the way of achieving this negation does not open the way for an affirmative drive according to a singular intensity (pleasure through X, for example). Exactly the opposite takes place in the feeling of the sublime: two intensities block each other. Despite the connection through a shared interest in the event, Lyotard's later concern with justice has brought him to the exact opposite of his earlier work, that is, to a renunciation of the movement afforded by intensities and to the primary aim of negation.

This does not mean that the later sense of the political cannot be viewed in a good light. Lyotard's resistance to Ideas of reason is given a positive and quite traditional context in the later chapters of *The Differend*. Resistance to Ideas is given a wider role in supporting democracy or the deliberative genre against the dominance of single views based on the hegemony of an Idea (however just it may appear at a given time). It is also given the role of defending minor narratives, that is, narratives that give identity to a people against Ideas, or meta-narratives that seek to legitimate a universal people or humanity. We can now see why Lyotard's philosophy of the differend is directed to the 'inhuman'. It has nothing to do with the libidinal materialist search for drives that cannot be thought of in terms of organic senses of the human being and the subject. Rather, the inhuman is the irreducible plurality of peoples and genres that must be defended against the totality understood in the Idea of humanity.

According to this contextual view of Lyotard's politics of the differend, an accusation often made against so-called postmodernism falls, at least in so far as it applies to him. It is not the case that he cannot and does not want to defend important modern institutions, above all democracy. It is that he sees those institutions as endangered more by efforts to reinforce them with Ideas such as humanity or meta-narratives of legitimation. So, in *The Differend*, while defining democracy in terms of a deliberative genre that allows all others to come into play through an 'Aristotelian and Kantian' model of dialectics, he also defines it in terms of a single end, that is, to have done with the differences at play in the debate: 'In the deliberative politics of modern democracies, the differend is exposed, even though the transcendental appearance of a single finality that would bring it to a resolution persists in helping to forget the differend, in making it bearable' (TD: 147).

Two possible sympathetic attitudes to democracy enter into conflict here. The first sees democracy as menaced from without by totalitarian politics and undermined from within by nihilistic positions that no longer subscribe to democratic values, hence weakening any capacity for defence. The second (Lyotard's) sees democracy as menaced from within by a coalition of Ideas of reason and meta-narratives that constitutes large parts of modern political ideology (for example, in the conjunction of the values of human rights, the arguments for their defence and furtherance within a given legal, economic and political structure, and historical accounts of why this defence is necessary and desirable). According to Lyotard, this coalition is exploited by capitalism and its capacity to thrive in systems where differences are maintained but subsumed under a general measure or set of norms. The first seeks to bolster the ideological and narrative strength of democracy ('These are the reasons for our universal ideas'; 'This is the account of why our values are legitimately universal'). However, Lyotard tries to resist this very tendency in favour of the fragility of a democracy free of any reason beyond its capacity to let differences come into play: 'The deliberative is more "fragile" than the narrative, it lets the abysses be perceived that separate genres of discourse from each other . . ., the abysses that threaten the social bond' (TD: 150).

However, The Differend is only a prolegomenon to the politics of the differend in that it does not seek to foster the feeling of the sublime in a treatment of Ideas and narratives. Instead, the book takes on a more reflective style, mixing close readings and interpretations with tentative aphorisms. The former demand a detached theoretical approach. The latter call for careful reflection and reconstruction. It could be claimed that this combination of aphorisms is itself a sign of the differend, that is, of an inability to construct a totality. This would be true if the aphorisms could not be combined in a coherent manner and if they instilled a sense of futility in the rational reader (something like the works of E. M. Cioran, for example). But this is not the case; if there is a swing from rational reconstruction to failure, it involves rational judgements against Lyotard, such as 'This argument is incomplete', as opposed to a sensation of the collapse of reason itself. The book is written as an invitation to follow an immanent thesis and set of arguments prior to judging any of the external cases or arguments that it applies to. The aphoristic style of The Differend is dialogical both between aphorisms and internally, with a strong emphasis on questions and answers and the economical pursuit of an argument across a wide range of topics and problems. We must look to the collections of essays that follow The Differend in order to find Lyotard searching for a style that puts the theoretical work into action. The main collections of essays, L'Inhumain and Moralités postmodernes (The Inhuman and Postmodern Fables), are where this takes place.

121

LYOTARD'S POSTMODERN IRONY

The solution Lyotard finds for putting his theory of the differend and the sublime into action concerns a shift in form and styles. This shift can be justified and explained on the basis of the connection of Ideas of reason and narratives of legitimation. When Ideas have to be applied to an actual group or population as opposed to a necessarily transcendental reason, the transfer takes place through narrative. A given population tells the story of how its norms and values come to represent the Idea *in concreto*. In *The Differend*, this process is described in the context of the 1789 Declaration of Rights. Lyotard argues that the declaration can never be legitimate for 'humanity' since it depends on a declaration (these are my/our rights) that can only be given by proxy by representatives: 'The splitting of the addressor of the Declaration into two entities, French nation and human being, corresponds to the equivocation of the declarative phrase: it presents a philosophical universe and co-presents a historical–political universe' (TD: 147).

The actual community or nation owes its identity to a shared narrative that includes an account of why it can stand in for humanity as a whole. But this account can never be legitimate, according to Lyotard, because any narrative of identity involves inclusions and exclusions. For a 'we' to emerge, there has to be a prior selection of who is allowed to tell the story of that 'we' and a prior understanding of how that story is to be told; this understanding cannot itself be justified by the narrative. His work on this argument takes place through the analysis of Cashinahua story-telling as reported by André-Marcel D'Ans in *Le dit des vrais hommes*. The problem with any narrative of a right to tell the story of a community is that it involves a circular structure: 'The Cashinahua narrator's authority to tell his stories is drawn from his name. His name, though, is authorized by his stories, especially those that recount the genesis of names' (TD: 155). So, in the case of the 1789 Declaration: 'The nation, inasmuch as it is a community, owes the essential of its consistency and authority to the traditions of names and narratives. These traditions are exclusivist. They imply borders and border conflicts. The legitimacy of a nation owes nothing to the idea of humanity and everything to the perpetuation of narratives of origin by means of repeated narrations' (147).

If Lyotard is to instil a disabling feeling around Ideas of reason as a means to a politics of resistance in actual cases, then the matter that he has to work on are the narratives that give the Idea actuality and allow it, if only unconsciously, to guide a further set of social acts. This is because the Idea in itself is not dubious so long as it remains transcendental. It only becomes dubious when applied in a specific case and, then, the application takes place through the medium of a narrative: 'The members of the Constituent Assembly would have been prey to a "transcendental appearance" and even perhaps to a *dementia*. They hallucinated humanity within the nation' (147). So the second task for his politics, after the isolation of the Ideas operative in a given community, is to identify and retell that often hidden and forgotten narrative. But this retelling must take on a very specific form, namely, one that rekindles the energising effect of the realisation that our vocation is to bring universal ideas into the actual, but that also makes us lose hope in the possibility of so doing. The form best suited to these twin tasks is irony, that is, as sincere as possible an evocation of the driving narrative accompanied by its almost imperceptible undoing.

The ironic form of Lyotard's later essays takes on many different styles, nearly all of which have been used by him over long periods. They include:

1   Reported dialogues between anonymous third-person male and female voices ('He'; 'She'): 'Can thought go on without a body', 'Interesting?';
2   Fictional short stories with an overtly philosophical lesson (morality tales): 'Marie goes to Japan', 'A postmodern fable';
3   Mannered, hyper-aesthetic exercises on common contemporary problems: 'Scapeland', 'Domus and the megalopolis', 'The zone';
4   Fragments and reflections provoked by problems in aesthetics or works of art: 'Newman: the instant', 'The sublime and the avant-garde', 'Something like communication without communication', 'Representation, presentation, unpresentable', 'Speech snapshot', 'After the sublime, the state of aesthetics', 'Conservation and colour', 'Obedience', 'Paradox on the graphic artist', 'A monument of possibles', 'Music mutic', 'Anima minima';
5   Dissertations on familiar philosophical themes, such as modernity, time and technology, but always with a view to contemporary concerns: 'Rewriting modernity', 'Matter and time', '*Logos* and *techne*, or telegraphy', 'Time today', 'God and the puppet';
6   Remarks on contemporary political, cultural and philosophical issues: 'The wall, the gulf, the system', '"The earth had no roads to begin with"', 'The general line', 'A bizarre partner', 'Directions to servants', 'Unbeknownst', 'The intimacy of terror'.

Quite often an essay juxtaposes these styles in order to reinforce the ironic effect or to correct a failure in irony. The categorisation above is therefore approximate and open to review, depending on what is taken to be the dominant style of a given essay.

The common thread that holds these styles together is the combination of great familiarity and strangeness. On the surface each of the essays goes over a well-known contemporary problem, such as 'Whither technological man?', teasing out essential theoretical or common-sense conclusions. These are then synthesised thanks to an Idea that we are not clearly conscious of, but that strikes us as fundamental once it is brought to our attention by

Lyotard. The Idea is usually something quite complex and sophisticated, such as 'We are brought together today by the human task of making sense of technology'. But this strong and convincing line of argument, based around a shared sense of what is occurring to us and why, is almost imperceptibly undermined by other suggestions. The operation of this suggestion takes many forms, and this explains the variety of styles. Each time, though, uncertainty and doubt are introduced often in a very short space or according to a variation in delivery. The problem for the reader is that this doubt grows on closer inspection: what can appear, at first, to be an incidental remark or lapse in style is, in fact, intricately woven into what appeared to be most familiar and clear-cut.

The sublime is a product of this technique: the moment of the attraction to the synthetic and purposeful power of the Idea is also a fall into feeling-induced incapacity. The simultaneity of attraction and repulsion is what characterises the sublime for Lyotard. This tension has to be directed to the Idea and to the actual cases that create the doubt. For instance, in his beautiful and troubling fictional dialogue on photographs taken of Charcot's hysterical patients, 'Speech snapshot', Lyotard attacks the typically Habermassian presupposition of an Idea of communication, that is, that all speech situations ideally presuppose a transfer of meaning. Lyotard shows that the supposition that all sensation-loaded human creations can, in principle, be given a meaning cannot live up to an encounter with the photographs:

> They were photographed to make an album of hysteria, so as to decipher what they might possibly be saying by these postures. Which implies this: that these bodily states were semantic elements and that they could be linked together by a syntax. One would thus obtain sentences, regulated sentences, and, along with them, meaning. But the photograph which was to make them speak produces an opposite impression on us. It fixes the states in their suspended instability, isolates them one from another, does not restore the syntax linking them. It makes us see tensorial stances.
>
> (IN: 132–3)

This passage cashes out the ironic dialogue that precedes it. The political power of Lyotard's work comes out well here. It forces us to allow the tension in our feelings with regard to the necessity of communication and the fact of lack of meaning to inhibit false forward movements based around the Idea. But the negative weakness of that work is also shown. Where can we go from here? We have been painfully discouraged from any meaning and, by extension, from other threads that could guide us on from the pictures. We have also been attracted to them for their negative power with respect to knowledge. The resulting frustration and discouragement is repeated through all of Lyotard's later essays. This itself reinforces their nihilistic impact. We are repeatedly drawn in, then dropped: 'The photo ceases to support the argumentation of the scientists, it suspends the dialectic (for an instant), unleashed tableau vivant. Grasp me if you can. But it will be or has been too early or too late' (134).

Nihilism aside, an internal problem with this approach is its tendency to failure because of the skills and knowledge it demands of its readers. I shall not spend much time addressing the different possible non-ironic interpretations of Lyotard's later thought. On the one hand, there is a simple first-order reading where the ironic function of the essay is simply missed and where the interpreter therefore stays with a given Idea as if it were correct. On this account, the later Lyotard appears to be an apologist for postmodern techno-science or the drive to go beyond what in the past may have counted as the fundamental human values and to embrace a super-human, highly technical and immaterial set of values. This reading misses his attempt to undermine such dreams by demonstrating their dependence on Ideas that themselves fail to apply convincingly to actual situations. Despite his work on the concept of the postmodern and on late modern and postmodern art, Lyotard's philosophy has never defended the naive postmodernism that aligns itself with late capitalism and modern technological advances.

On the other hand, there is a reading perhaps overly attuned to Lyotard's work on the event that sees the later essays as moves into a strongly ethical stance. On this reading, the work on narratives of legitimation, on Ideas of reason and on actual aspects of contemporary science, technology, philosophy, economics and politics, is strictly critical. Strict in the sense that it can divest itself of any positive attachment to them and instead argue for an alternative position. This would be the philosophy of resistance to modern Ideas and contemporary culture, politics and economics in the name of the event, of what cannot be represented according to those ideas and within those contemporary structures. This is a more plausible position, if only because it can cite many important passages where Lyotard closes essays on the idea of testifying to that which cannot be represented but which has an inestimable value for that very reason. For example in 'The general line', dedicated to Gilles Deleuze, he makes the following claim: 'If humanity does not preserve the inhuman region in which we can meet this or that which completely escapes the exercise of rights, we do not merit the rights that we have been recognised' (PF: 121).

The passage quoted above cannot be read as a simple apology for an 'inhuman region' without cancelling Lyotard's most consistent arguments concerning how to preserve that which escapes rights or Ideas. Resistance can only take place through a positive attraction to modern Ideas and to their possible actualisation. It is necessary to embrace them in order to become simultaneously aware of their failure. If there is an inhuman region, it is always dependent on the feeling of the sublime, perhaps extended to other feelings of simultaneous attraction and repulsion from Ideas. There cannot be an ethics or philosophy of the event and 'the unpresentable'; only a pragmatics of the feeling of the sublime.

It is also important to distinguish Lyotard's use of irony and the sublime against Ideas of reason from the postmodern irony adopted by Richard Rorty in *Contingency, Irony, Solidarity*. For Lyotard, irony is a tool for releasing the sublime against Ideas. It is not a position in itself – one that is meant to allow modern institutions to be prolonged free of modern claims to universality in terms of norms and values. Politically, the two thinkers share a resistance to universality. But Lyotard's position is much tighter in terms of what it applies to – Ideas – and how it undermines them – the sublime. The price of this methodological coherence is a nihilism that makes the claim that he is supporting or refining liberal democracy impossible to sustain. This may also be the case for Rorty, but the reasons will be different.

THE INHUMAN

If the ironic form of Lyotard's essays is not primary in terms of his later politics, the selection of the actual cases that turn back our enthusiasm for given Ideas of reason is important and distinctive. I have divided these cases into two categories: the inhuman and matter. This is a somewhat contingent division and selection of headings, since the cases cannot be seen to give rise to a new set of concepts opposed to given Ideas of reason without undermining the whole project of the later essays. It would make no sense to speak of Lyotard's philosophy of the inhuman or of matter, for this would be to reintroduce the type of thinking by leading Ideas or concepts that he seeks to resist. So, although the titles and headings chosen to characterise his later thought have and will continue to provide a welcome way of organising a disparate set of essays, this must not lead to a conceptual systematisation of the cases he deploys against Ideas. Instead, there is only a philosophy that exploits the contingent power certain events have in triggering feelings in a given situation. In this section, I will discuss the events grouped loosely under the banner 'The inhuman'. The following section will tackle 'Matter'.

Lyotard releases inhuman events into his texts against the collection of Ideas that collectively contribute to the contemporary Idea of the human. It is important to stress the time-bound aspect of the contribution and the approach to inhumanity in a non-essentialist and non-transcendental manner. For him, the human is relative not only in its resistance to absolute definitions but also in its constant reassessment through the different ways in which it provides an umbrella for Ideas. So he does not deny that essential and transcendental definitions of the human are crucial components of our Idea of the human. But he does not accept that they offer the last word on the Idea in its capacity to provide a powerful thread to contemporary thought.

For example, one of the dominant Ideas discussed in the later essays is 'The human must not be earth-bound' or, more formally, 'The human is inorganic'. At first sight, there appears to be little connection between these Ideas and the Kantian definition given in the previous chapter, because of the apparently sensible properties 'earth-bound' and 'inorganic'. These ought to be seen as concepts of the understanding that can be verified through an appeal to sensible intuitions. But Lyotard raises them to an ideal level by making them horizons of an abstract thought-process. This process begins, first, with the observed depletion of earthly resources, but this is then reasoned to the abstract limit of the end of the world as providing a viable environment for human life. Second, actual research into non-organic systems that exhibit human capacities such as thought is reasoned to the limit of a wholly non-organic human.

Two actual fields – concern with the environment and research into artificial intelligence – have their contemporary intellectual dominance explained through an appeal to an Idea of reason. They give it its power within the more general idea of the human, while it allows us to organise them and make sense of what they mean for us. In fact, according to Lyotard, this sense is constructed out of a shared relation at the level of the Idea: the research into the inorganic is a response to the depletion of resources. The Idea is then only given its full strength when the myth or narrative of the end of the world is also a narrative of a renewal of human life elsewhere; this is the postmodern fable from the essay of the same name: 'All of this research turns out, in fact, to be dedicated, closely or from afar, to testing and remodelling the so-called human body, or to replacing it, in such a way that the brain remains able to function with the aid only of the energy resources available in the cosmos. And so was prepared the final exodus of the negentropic system far from earth' (PF: 91).

The point here is not to determine whether Lyotard is ultimately right in his isolation of this particular Idea and narrative. This would lead to the fatuous journalistic discussion of the importance of science fiction, political speeches on the twenty-first century, apocalyptic movements and so on. At this stage, his work is pragmatic to the extent that right is replaced by a practical demand: 'In so far as an Idea may hold sway, has its power been deflected?' It is at least reasonable to observe that cultural products that merge ideas concerning the human, artificial intelligence, space exodus and the end of the world have some popularity and are given prominence by some (*2001: A Space Odyssey*, for instance). These products are a sign that Lyotard has some justification in supposing that Ideas concerning a non-organic future provide a guiding thread for thinking about the future for humanity; here is the ironic version he proposes for it in 'Time today':

The human race is already in the grip of the necessity of having to evacuate the solar system in 4.5 billion years. It will have been the transitory vehicle for an extremely improbable process of com-plexification. The exodus is already on the agenda. The only chance of success lies in the species adapting itself to the complexity of what challenges it. And if the exodus succeeds, what it will have preserved is not the species itself but the 'most complete monad' with which it was pregnant.

(IN: 65)

Lyotard gives this account in such a way that it is shadowed by the realisation that the human is not what is preserved or of value in this Idea of a non-organic human future. For example, in 'A postmodern fable' he debunks his own version of the narrative that underpins the Idea by analysing it in terms of a double mistake on the human. The narrative owes nothing to a human historicity. It is a physical history 'concerned only with energy and matter as a state of energy' (98). It is not a history of past, present and future where the capacity of human consciousness holds past and future in a privileged present. It is a history of energy where the present of energy does not preserve the past or anticipate the future: 'As for the events ("it happened that . . .") that punctuate the fabulous history of energy, the latter neither awaits not retains them'. The history has no end, in the sense of a longed-for emancipation; it is merely a passage from one material state to a more complex one, with no sense of value other than growth in complexity. Finally, the history does not allow for hope, a better future belonging 'to a subject of history who promises him/herself – or to whom has been promised – a final perfection' (99).

So the irony of Lyotard's thesis regarding the Idea of the human as a bet on a non-organic future is that the narrative that brings this idea to life for us is dehumanised. It is a postmodern fable in that it is shorn of human meaning whilst still maintaining the form of modern teleological narratives: 'For lack of an eschatology, the conjugated, the conjugated mechanicalness and contingency of the story it tells leave thought suffering for a lack of finality. This suffering is the postmodern state of thought, what is by agreement called in these times its crisis, its malaise, or its melancholia' (100). A first sense of the inhuman in his later essays is therefore a rather banal and familiar remark on the rationalisation of the human and its environment through technology (IN: 69–73). It only goes beyond this familiarity in ironically pointing out just how far this process has moved into thought, even concerning the Ideas most central to modern humanist politics and philosophy.

But this does not imply that Lyotard's deployment of irony against Ideas falls into a simple contradiction regarding its democratic motivation to further debate by opposing the dominant role of universal Ideas. It can sometimes appear that he is not only using the melancholia that results from the realisation of the end of humanity in technology, but that he views it as the only possible reaction to this process. Sometimes he invites this conclusion; the later the essay, the more true this appears to be ('With no cognitive or ethical pretension, the fable grants itself a poetic or aesthetic status. It has worth only by its faithfulness to the postmodern affection, melancholia' (PF: 101)). This would imply that there was no point to democratic debate since all human aims must ultimately lead to melancholia and disaffection. But Lyotard's use of irony cannot be given this single affective goal. He wants to dash the Idea, and to that extent he wants melancholia. On the other hand, the way in which he negates the attraction of Ideas of reason points to an affirmative aspect of his later philosophy.

The inhuman is not only that which, in the form of technology and rationalisation, destroys the Idea of the survival of humanity from within. It is also that which resists the dominance of that negative inhumanity. There are therefore two senses of the inhuman at work in Lyotard's later essays. The one he seeks to affirm is not inhuman in the sense of overly determined and mechanistic systems that lack human feelings and affects, as well as human reason in the sense of that which provides a teleology and order for those affects and feelings. It is inhuman in the sense of a reserve from or a beyond of reason and technology. This sense links essays from *The Inhuman* and *Postmodern Fables* to his most careful definitions of the postmodern in 'Answering the question: What is the postmodern?' included in the English translation of *La Condition postmoderne* (1979b; English translation 1984c). Properly, the postmodern in art, philosophy and literature is that which disturbs an emerging order in them. It does so by lending an ear to, and expressing, that which cannot be incorporated into the order and yet that which allows for its emergence.

In an essay from *The Inhuman*, 'Rewriting modernity', Lyotard explains this disturbance and the matter it works with through the practice of 'rewriting'. This is related to the Freudian psychoanalytical technique of working through (*Durcharbeitung*) in the way in which it seeks to reactivate an originary, but not original, unconscious event. Postmodern art and literature involve a suggested recollection (an anamnesis) of that which gives modern art its creative potential and intensity, but also that which it denies as it becomes settled and well ordered: 'Rewriting, as I mean it here, obviously concerns the anamnesis of the Thing. Not only that Thing that starts off a supposedly "individual" singularity, but of the thing that haunts the "language", the tradition and the material with, against and in which one writes' (33). By definition, this view of the postmodern is a resistance to categorisation and to its own categorisation, a point that Lyotard has to labour because of his association with the category of the postmodern ('What I've here called rewriting clearly has nothing to do with what is called postmodernity or postmodernism on the market of contemporary ideologies') (34).

This means that rewriting works with the same 'materials' and in the same direction as the art, politics and philosophy of the inhuman outlined in its positive sense above. The direction is against reason, defined as the elimination of the disturbing and unpredictable power of feelings and affects, and against technology, defined as instrumental moves towards increased performance and complexity. This alliance of reason and technology is that which the postmodern seeks to work through in the modern: 'Postmodernity is not a new age, but the rewriting of some of the features claimed by modernity, and first of all modernity's claim to ground its legitimacy on the project of liberating humanity as a whole through science and technology' (34). To the extent that modern works also seek to do this in their tradition they can be counted as postmodern (or the reverse): 'But as I have said, that rewriting has been at work, for a long time now, in modernity itself.'

If the direction here is clear and indeed rather unoriginal, the materials for following it are very hard to pin down, though they alone can make the effort stand out from the proliferation of doubts about modern 'techno-science'. In Lyotard's definitions of the postmodern and the inhuman, there is a split between a return to Freud and the matter of the unconscious and a use of Kant and the sublime. On the one hand, the practice of suggested recollection seems to indicate a work on a specific unconscious matter that underlies order in art, Ideas and so on. This recollection aims to release affects in the sense of using them to indicate and work through tensions within order. This is exactly what Lyotard does in using irony to allow what Ideas conceal within themselves to work slowly to the surface.

The recollection, however, does not work directly on affects but on the matter shared by depth and surface: language as the form of communication. By experimenting on the form of language in the many different ways outlined above, his irony can allow doubt to creep into order. This form, in its openness to experimentation, is that which leaves the Idea open to a return of the affect: 'Being prepared to receive what thought is not prepared to think is what deserves the name of thinking. As I have said, this attitude is to be found in reputedly rational language as much as in the poetic, in art, ordinary language, if, that is, it is essential to the cognitive discourse to progress' (IN: 73).

On the other hand, away from this definition of the inhuman as a relation between affect and order through a form that makes both possible, Lyotard also defines the inhuman in terms of the Kantian sublime. In this case, the affects are not involved in a transference or interference through form. They are involved in the determination and communication of a limit to order, a point on which it depends but that it cannot capture or represent. The difference is between two types of resistance, though Lyotard often passes from one to the other because they share a pragmatic aesthetic response to the problem of how to resist. The avant-garde in art, politics or philosophy has to be concerned with form and affects.

But, in the case of the sublime, resistance is in the name of an impossibility, that is, in the event as sublime feeling lies the limit of the claims of reason: 'The question mark of the Is it happening? stops. With the occurrence, the will is defeated. The avant-gardist task remains that of undoing the presumption of the mind with respect to time. The sublime feeling is the name of this privation' ('The sublime and the avant-garde': 107). Whereas, in the case of anamnesis, resistance is in the name of an interference, that is, a passage of intense affects from matter, the rich form of language, to the order of a language overly determined by science and technology: 'At a level below languages, works, institutions, always lying latent beneath the audible but never covered by it, this breath does not speak, it moans, it mutters' (PF: 224).

What is implied by this divide in definitions of the inhuman as disturbing matter or disabling limit? The latter is entirely consistent with the aim of resiting the Idea through an appeal to the sublime. The inhuman is the sublime itself in the way it indicates that Ideas of reason cannot be presented:

> The sublime is not a pleasure, it is a pleasure of pain: we fail to present the absolute, and that is a displeasure, but we know that we have to present it, that the faculty of feeling or imagining is called on to bring about the sensible (the image). To present what reason can conceive, and even if it cannot manage to do this, and we suffer from this, a pure pleasure is felt from this.
>
> ('Representation, presentation, unpresentable': 126)

The inhuman is the limit of the human, thought according to the absolute. It is therefore not a thing or a matter, but that which resists all attempts to close on any given Idea or definition of the human. As such, the political thought of in terms of the inhuman falls prey to the critical conclusions drawn at the end of the previous chapter. It is a political attitude that closes itself off from others, in the sense of a severance from other forms of politics and discourse. The politics limits the human, but it cannot interact with it. It has no consistency or reliability; it lives and dies with the sublime, a feeling that cannot be preserved in forms of discourse that seeks to represent it. Finally, the political defence of the inhuman has no cause other than itself. It does not stand for anything, not even differends.

A possible objection to these conclusions concerns the possible role played by a politics of the inhuman in a wider democratic context. The inhuman would be a particular voice within a wider democratic debate and as such would not be cut off from a wider political context that would give it consistency and a more general cause. But how would a politics dependent on feelings participate in the debate? By definition, the inhuman cannot be identified with a given cause or represented within a debate. So, even if the point of a politics based on the sublime is to use that feeling to limit Ideas of reason in their role within democratic debate by triggering it in participants to that debate, this is a transference of the limits of that politics to them. They cannot do anything with the inhuman other than deploy it again in a similar fashion. This raises the danger of a seizure of the political in the face of the sublime. Political debate and action would become reduced to a testimony to the lack of validity of Ideas of reason. This would deliver politics to an ever-decreasing capacity to justify positive acts and to the negative grip of the feeling of the sublime.

The role of Lyotard's later essays within a wider politics suggested at the start of this essay is an impossible one, because there is no possible inter-action between resistance and a wider politics other than negative moves of limitation and disabling. The problem of nihilism cannot be overcome in a philosophy that cannot posit anything beyond negation and limitation: 'Matter does not question the mind, it has no need of it, it exists, or rather *insists*, it sists "before" questioning and answer, 'outside' them. It is presence as unpresentable to the mind, always withdrawn from its grasp. It does not offer itself to dialogue and dialectic' (IN: 142).

MATTER

Further objections to these unfavourable conclusions come out of Lyotard's later essays on the relation between art and matter. The limiting function of the feeling of the sublime is balanced by a positive attraction to matter, defined as that which artists and thinkers can exploit in a creative manner in order to testify to the limits of Ideas through the sublime. The politics of Lyotard's later essays would then be about a sensitivity to matter as well as about an ironic undermining of Ideas of reason. The nihilism implied in the latter would be answered by the affirmation of matter in a similar way to his much earlier use of an active passivity to intensity in the libidinal philosophy. It often seems that the later essays hark back to Lyotard's early work on art and politics, bypassing the dead-end of his search of judgement and justice in the sublime: 'Perhaps words themselves, in the most secret place of thought, are its matter, its timbre, its nuance, i.e. what it cannot manage to think. Words "say", sound, touch, always "before" thought. And they always "say" something other than what thought signifies, and what it wants to signify by putting them into form' (IN: 142).

This view seems to find support in the inventiveness and insight into space and architecture in the most artistic of Lyotard's later essays ('Scapeland' and 'Domus and the megapole'). In these essays, he writes on space as landscape and dwelling place so as to release new and disturbing ways of thinking about our relation to what we see and where we live – ways that are politically liberating in the sense of displacing familiar values and norms about nature, the city and the home. For example, in 'Scapeland', Lyotard

132

moves from a study of the organising principles at work in our relation to a landscape to a reflection on the relation to the face as landscape. A similar organisation comes into play when we have perceived the face as a whole as when we take in a site as landscape. We can move through both according to familiar laws and values: 'It is only "after" it has been a landscape, but also while it is still a landscape, that the face is covered over by a countenance and uncovers the countenance. The INNOCENCE of walking in it is forgotten. Prescriptions begin to come and go between you and me' (190). A possible art of the face would then be to free parts of the face, its flesh, its colour from organisation in order to release new possibilities, new connections, new ways of thinking. This move harks back to similar moments concerning flesh and body parts in *Libidinal Economy* ('Gaze of an eye, slow, thoughtless, fixed, then in a flash the head pivots so that there is no more than a profile, Egypt' (29).

This return to libidinal philosophy can also be found in the main references of *The Inhuman* and *Postmodern Fables*. Lyotard reflects again through Cézanne, Duchamp and John Cage. But each time, where the early work stresses a conducting of intensities through matter and a trans-formation of structures, the later work stresses a reduced, negative set of intensities and a failure of structures to grasp the event of that intensity. For example, in the most nuanced of Lyotard's later essays on art and affects, 'Anima minima', he studies the minimal state of an affect that reduces the soul to a registering of a material change and nothing more: 'The *anima* exists only as affected. Sensation, whether likeable or detestable, also announces to the *anima* that it would not even be, that it would remain inanimate, had nothing affected it' (243). In the libidinal philosophy, as in this late essay, this passive state is all-important. But in 'Anima minima' it is not actively pursued through and for the transformation of structures but in and for itself. When intensity occurs it is as a negation of the minimal soul: 'The soul comes into its existence dependent on the sensible, thus violated, humiliated . . . Even while the event brings the soul into life, casts it into the living heart of pain and/or pleasure, no matter how carried away it might be, the soul remains caught between the terror of its impending death and the horror of its servile existence' (244).

After *The Differend*, matter has become that which arrests our faculties and which stops them overreaching themselves. The artist must bear witness to these limits by presenting matter so that it may reduce the subject to a hung state between activity and destruction: 'Art, writing, give grace to the soul condemned to the penalty of death, but in such a way as not to forget it' (245). If Lyotard is right in describing the affect of matter as an arrest that must be testified to in art, then this is a different turn away from his early work than the need for judgement discussed in the previous chapter. The claim would be that the active passivity of the libidinal philosophy was still dependent on the imposition of an illegitimate structure that hid a more profound matter. The arrested soul as 'the minimal condition of aesthetics' is given a comprehensive role in the later work; it has claims over all structures: 'It would suspend not only the prejudgments of the world and of substance but also those of subjectivity and of life' (249).

However, from the point of view of the main concept of the libidinal philosophy, dissimulation, the mistake lies in the idea that matter has this all-inhibiting hold on other structures through the simultaneity of terror and delight. In the soul-oriented language of 'Anima minima', Lyotard describes this hold thus: 'The *anima* is threatened with privation: speech, light, sound, life would be absolutely lacking. That's *terror*. Suddenly the threat is lifted, the terror lifted, it's *delight*' (245). The description of matter as sublime in its most raw relation to sensation presupposes that structures are not necessary for matter to cause affects. But the combination of sensations described in the sublime (terror and delight, pleasure and pain) are dependent on con-tingent structures. There is no necessary relation that holds between the structures associated with expectation and those associated with the fear that nothing may occur. So there is no necessity to the sublimity of a given thing. Not all spectators are rendered silent by a Barnett Newman painting. There can be patterns of behaviour and artistic creation that break the bond of pleasure and pain in the sublime. Lyotard admits as much when he makes distinctions between sublime and non-sublime art. For Kant, however, the Savoyard peasant who 'unhesitatingly called all lovers of snow-mountains fools' (115) can at least in principle become subject to the sublime power of the mountains. This is because the sublime depends on a shared human nature that makes the sublime equally shareable (116).

In the concept of dissimulation, Lyotard suggests that intensity must work through structures and that their relation has no necessary features. His politics then deploys principles for an active passivity that allows intensity to be conducted through as many structures as possible, thereby exploiting its polymorphous quality. This politics is also subversive of the later work on the sublime, in particular where it can be reduced to a claim for a privileged region best adapted to the occurrence of the feeling of the sublime. Any such region is always in contact with others and is always open to intensities other than the sublime, would be the claim of the early work. Lyotard claims, in 'Anima minima', that there is a pure aesthetic event that has a special and disabling effect on a minimal, but essential aesthetic 'soul': 'The *aistheton* is an event; the soul exists only if that event stimulates it; when it is lacking, the soul is dissipated into the nothingness of the inanimate' (245). This claim is false from the point of view of libidinal economy because any event takes place in many structures. The event of intensity disturbs each of these and rearranges its internal configuration.

7

CONCLUSION.
A WITHDRAWAL FROM
THE POLITICAL?

NOSTALGIA AND ANAMNESIS

> In two centuries, and whatever the case might be with the
> theme of the sublime, the nihilist problematics from which it
> proceeds is diffused into every treatment, literary and artistic,
> of the sensible. Nihilism does not just end the efficiency of the
> great narratives of emancipation, it does not just lead to the
> loss of values and the death of God, which render metaphysics
> impossible. It casts suspicion on the data of aesthetics.
>
> (PF: 245)

The two dominant and most consistent political positions to come out of
Lyotard's struggle with nihilism are the passive politics of *Libidinal
Economy* and the activation of the feeling of the sublime against Ideas of
reason in *The Differend*. I have argued that the former is more successful
than the latter in escaping a fundamental reliance on negation, because it
has an affirmative orientation with respect to feelings and desires defined as
libidinal intensities. According to Lyotard's definition of nihilism in
Libidinal Economy, this fundamental activity of negation and limitation
involves a turn away from intensities, the affects that can disturb and
reinvigorate a moribund structure. Given that the turn is fundamental, the
drift away from this reinvigoration is final and the greatest danger then
becomes a hopeless reflection on this endless deferral. So, even if a philosophy is based on the power of feelings against structures, as is the case in
Lyotard's later philosophy, this philosophy can still be nihilistic.

When affects are still thought of in terms of a fundamental negative
structure, such as the connection of attraction and repulsion in a negation
of one another and in a negation of activity according to Ideas of reason
in the sublime, then it will still fall prey to nihilism. The melancholic tone
and attitude to aesthetic events in Lyotard's later essays is testament to

135

this process. No novel thread can be followed that allows for the negative alliance of pleasure, pain and inactivity to be broken. Works of art were once a site for a revolutionary conduction of affects through structures; they triggered disturbing feelings and desires that set structures in motion. Now they bear testimony to a delayed disaster described in 'Anima minima': 'Works of art are charged with honouring this miraculous and precarious condition. Timbre, idiom, nuance are not solicited for their face value, for the immediate sense the body and culture grant them. They must be burnt-out witnesses of an imminent and "delayed" disaster, as Marcel Duchamp used to say. And there is no poetics for regulating the manner of bearing witness, nor an aesthetics to tell how it should be received' (PF: 245).

The paradox that prevents this passage from leading to a positive politics lies in the activities of honouring and bearing witness. How can these activities acquire even a minimal degree of consistency through time without cancelling out any of the energy necessary for that task? With the lack of rules or poetics and the lack of structural sense, all that can be transmitted from one instance of honouring to another is delay or postponement. So, aside from a chance occurrence of a sublime event, a politics planned around or for those events is nothing but an affirmation of a past failure to honour and to testify. This is because there is no memory or representation of the moment when we are grasped by a sublime event that succeeds in carrying its combination of feelings of attraction and repulsion, of a 'delayed disaster'. When that combination is represented, the power to represent is that which is saved from the disaster; it gives meaning through a cognitive continuity. But that continuity is lost in the event proper – perhaps above all. All that is memorised or represented is a negation of the act of bearing witness. A politics based on the repetition of this negation cannot remain active for long.

However, at least one possibility remains for Lyotard's later politics. This would be that the continuity that it requires is not based on memory as representation and on a politics of a conscious activity of honouring and bearing witness. Instead, the politics would itself be set by a feeling that extends through time, nostalgia, and a strategy allied to it, anamnesis or suggested recollection. He raises this possibility in a number of the essays in *Postmodern Fables*, notably 'The zone' and 'Anima minima'. Nostalgia is perhaps the dominant tone of his last works; it is what remains after their work of ironic undermining. In the latter of the two essays, the one that engages most closely with the impossibility of a politics of the sublime, Lyotard concludes by attempting to argue for a 'temperament' that responds to a statement. This statement appears finally to break off the feeling of the sublime from any possibility of memory: '"A brief feeling is born from an event, itself issuing forth from nothing"; only an *archi-epoche* of sensation could perhaps enunciate this proposition. It would suspend not only the prejudgments of this world and of substance but also those of subjectivity and of life' (249). We cannot remember the event and all it leaves us with is a nostalgia for its passing.

So, even though the minimal soul in the grip of the sublime is 'to be thought as being without memory', this is to be seen as a discontinuity in terms of what it can carry forward with it as knowledge ('What comes back in this time to come is not located in the time of clocks and consciences, and it is not worth remembering'). But there is a continuity in that 'what is to come, comes forth as a coming back'. What this means is that the feeling of the sublime occurs as a return, in the sense of being accompanied by a feeling that something lost has returned in a different form. The feeling of the sublime is then not a remembering of a positive thing; it is an attraction to a past thing without knowledge of it: 'That is why [the artistic gesture of annihilation] always induces a nostalgia and motivates an anamnesis' (translation slightly modified, the original translation by Georges Van Den Abeele gives 'amnesia' for '*anamnèse*'). The consistency of a politics of the sublime would then come from the requirement to look back on the past as something that cannot simply be remembered, but as something that must still be reworked in the sense of a Freudian suggested recollection.

A politics of nostalgia and anamnesis that may take off from the later essays and from the book on Heidegger, *Heidegger and 'the Jews'*, is not the modern nostalgia discussed here in Chapter 3 in the discussion between Derrida and Lyotard – a nostalgia for apodicticity and totality. It is rather the task of reworking the past so as to make us feel an unavoidable loss. The past must be felt to return but only as something that cannot be recuperated and handled fully in the present. It is therefore a testimony to the way in which the present annihilates the past. The art-work, the strongest political act, would then be a reminder of the failure of the present to capture a past that conditions it. This would not be a conservative nostalgia, in the sense of a search for a past that could and ought to be brought back into the present. It is rather a way of reminding ourselves of the limits – the law – that bind any action in the present. We must work in the shadow of events that we cannot finally have done with or represent.

The event that conditions Lyotard's nostalgia and anamnesis most strongly is Auschwitz. The minimalist and abstract art-works by Liebeskind and Whiteread, for example, would be part of a struggle against the hegemony of representation in our media-dominated reflection on history: '[Abstraction, minimalism] continue to testify "after Auschwitz" to the impossibility for art and writing to testify for the Other' (*Heidegger et 'les juifs'*: 83–4). Once again, impossibility is fundamental to what Lyotard understands as nostalgia and anamnesis. How can they be repeated in different situations, that they then connect, without elevating the impossibility to the position of single most important aspect of a politics? How could that politics survive as an activity that went beyond singular instances of nostalgia? Lyotard's working through the past is nihilistic and subject to the same contradictions as the politics of the sublime: 'All that I can do is tell how I can no longer even tell the story' (81). Once this becomes everything, then there can be no way of ensuring a future even for these acts.

There is no nostalgia or drive to rework the past in the libidinal philosophy. Active passivity is defined, first, in terms of positive principles that allow for chance connections and intensities to guide our actions (seek powerlessness in the blurring of borders between what is discussed and the theory that discusses it, multiply principles of enunciation, and invite failure into discourse). Second, it is defined in terms of negative principles that guide us away from the activities of free subjects, from self-identity and from the selection of affects (do not will as a free subject, seek anonymity by abandoning analysis, do not believe that affects can be chosen). The turn to the past could not therefore be willed. Neither could nostalgia be preserved as that which gives continuity to our actions. A nostalgic reworking would be one of the structures that could grasp us. But, as soon as it did, the principles of active passivity would push for its demotion as a structure that guided our activity, as a primary and isolated structure, as a structure that we could choose, that ought to mean something for us and that defined which affects were noble and worth selecting.

Does this simply amount to a withdrawal from the political, defined as a positive engagement with political bodies, issues and theory? Do the principles of active passivity allow for critical work against a given state and for a better one? Do they allow for a political struggle on a particular issue, for rights and against discrimination and injustice, for example? Could they form the basis for a political ideology that could define and give guidance to a political group, to a nation or to humanity? The activity in active passivity is for passivity, not in the sense of a specific passive state such as a religious doctrine and attitude, but in the sense of a radical openness to chance and to multiplicity. That activity is also against our most familiar bases for political activity: subjects, identities, specific passions. So, even if we were to stress that active passivity is not a lack of action, it is still a strict restriction of activity to passivity.

This restriction is the key to understanding why this politics escapes nihilism. It does not actively pursue, work through or work against well-defined institutions, goals, identities. But neither does it turn away from such activities and into a silence of no action and of no basis for action. These remain in the situations that we are involved in and in the way in which we seek to allow chance to have a hand in their transformation. Active passivity is not a denial of the importance and intensity of the political structures that define a given situation. On the contrary, these are the material it has to work on in terms of introducing chance encounters and eliminating the belief in greater control of political structures through the subject, self-identity and selection. The point will never be to eliminate political structures. The main concept of libidinal economy, dissimulation, implies that structures are always necessary. But, equally, they are always open to the unpredictable occurrence of intensities. Libidinal economy is a strategy that seeks to loosen structures and to open them up to new possibilities defined as new connections with other structures through the unpredictable occurrence of intensities defined as feelings and desires.

The strategy does not itself have a goal that can be chosen, in the sense of guaranteed or defined in terms of the exact connections and transformation it involves. So, even though there is no withdrawal from the political in the sense of always having to work with political bodies, issues and theories, there is a withdrawal in the sense of seeking to act within these bodies with no idea of the exact consequences of our actions. But even this is not to pull back from well-determined actions, since the search for chance is given in the positive principles of the blurring of borders, of multiplicity and failure, and the negative principles against free choice, self-analysis and the selection of affects. Libidinal economists work with what is given, in terms of the structures that organise the intensities that grasp them. They work in a positive way with respect to those structures, in the sense of seeking to allow them to change. However, they cannot plot or promise the outcome of that change. They are not nihilists because they affirm their intensities and the structures that organise them by inviting further intensities and transformations of structure. That invitation is not a negation of that which is opened up to new possibilities because it cannot be judged negatively with respect to what may be to come, since it is not defined.

This allows us to interpret the last lines of *Libidinal Economy* as a response to the problem of the withdrawal from familiar senses of the political generated by a philosophical fear of nihilism:

> What would be interesting would be to stay put, but quietly seize every chance to function as good intensity-conducting bodies. No need for declarations, manifestos, organizations, provocations, no need for exemplary actions. Set dissimulation to work on behalf of intensities. Invulnerable conspiracy, headless, homeless, with neither programme nor project, deploying a thousand cancerous tensors in the bodies of signs. We invent nothing, that's it, yes, yes, yes, yes.

(262)

There is no withdrawal, in the sense of a flight to a place remote from political situations. We must 'stay put'. Neither is there a withdrawal in the sense of refusing to work through traditional political institutions, so long as their goals and methods are not taken as final. Instead, familiar political structures (declarations, manifestos, organisations, programmes and projects) are sites within which we must follow the principles of active passivity in order to allow new, destabilising intensities to occur. So 'the political' is necessary but not primary. It is a contingent context and not a ground.

Lyotard's invulnerability is then defined with respect to nihilism in all its traditional political guises. Nihilism is introduced with the negations implicit in the different identities defined by declarations, manifestos and organisations. It is implied by the endlessly deferred goals of programmes and projects, with their dependence upon utopian signs: freedom, truth, peace and justice. It is also present in the illusions of starting from or arriving back to a home, or being guided by and fighting for a leader. Failure, defined as the moment when one feels or becomes conscious of the futility of the political structures that have been adopted as the core of our identity, is not a threat for Lyotard's active passivity. It invites that failure as an ally in the triggering of intensity and movement within structures – this is what makes it invulnerable.

A POLITICS FOR WHOM?

However, even if it is the case that Lyotard does not simply turn his back on traditional senses of the political, would not a general active passivity imply a terrible end to that politics? *Libidinal Economy* is written as if it is for a minority ('we libidinal economists') whose existence is made possible by the role of conspirators. They work within capitalism for the power of intensities. Their identity is fleeting since it is defined by events that are beyond their control, though they are cleared by the search for passivity. But the principles of such an activity do not have an in-built restriction to a limited group. The work on libidinal economy is not easily accessible, but neither is it a form of esotericism. So what happens if we all become conspirators? A general conspiracy appears to be a contradiction, since there would be nobody to conspire against. Would not this lead rapidly to an absence of political structures through an absence of people prepared to uphold them? Where would intensities occur then? Do not subversive and seditious feelings and desires depend on complex structures of laws, inclusions, exclusions, categorisations?

The answer to these questions lies in a precision of the question 'For whom?' In Lyotard's libidinal philosophy, the 'whom' could never be 'people', that is, well-defined political actors. The generalisation that goes from a small group to all actors is beside the point in terms of the principles of active passivity and in terms of the relation of intensities to structures. There is nothing transcendent of intensity and structure, such as the essential human subject or soul. Neither are intensity and structure susceptible to a transcendental analysis, for example, where the development of structure and the experience of intensity are shown to presuppose subjectivity and intentionality.

Of course, these bald assertions only serve to explain why the reference to actors is not taken to be the right approach; they are not arguments as such. Indeed, no final arguments are given against transcendence and the transcendental. As I have argued in Chapter 3, the form of Lyotard's arguments is such that specific positions that depend on a transcendent human essence are analysed and shown to be unsatisfactory only within accounts of how intensities affect a specific given thing. Lyotard attempts to show the following, but always in practice. Things do not 'happen to' W. Instead, the structures V, V', V" that organise and exploit intensities – note how the short-hand for feelings and desires is misleading at this point – are rearranged into different structures W, W', W" by the unforeseeable occurrence of an unmanageable intensity. Neither does the activity A 'make the structure' X, or 'accomplish the act' Y, or 'determine the phenomenon' Z. Instead, X becomes X' because of the occurrence of intensities. The act Y must be explained in terms of the structures and intensities involved. The phenomenon Z presupposes a relation of intensities and structures and nothing more.

For example, in *Libidinal Economy*, Lyotard transforms the concept of the labyrinth, developed in terms of a series of examples, in order to destabilise a reliance on the subject or subjectivity. He seeks to show how the pattern of events that come to make up a path through a labyrinth are not explained well in terms of conscious decisions by a free subject. He also seeks to show that the same holds true for the assumption that subjectivity, defined as a capacity to act, is presupposed by the path. Instead, the pattern of events is resistant to meaning and not only in the senses of actions by something for something and of a meaningful activity, communication, for example. It is also resistant to the attempt to decipher a true objective meaning for the path or even a trend towards a final meaning (including the collection and organisation of every past meaning attributed to the path): 'No-one has the power to draw up the map of the great film; this, seen from the outside (but it has no outside) would be some kind of monstrous beast whose constitutive parts would change according to unpredictable modulations, would appear and disappear with the same terrifying ease as virtual images on a screen' (LE; 36).

For Lyotard, the labyrinth does not pre-exist the events that take place in it. Instead, each time there is an event, defined as the occurrence of an intensity, new structures (labyrinths) appear alongside pre-existing ones, changing their relation to each other and their relation to the new event understood as meaningful. So there is no continuity, in terms of sense or meaning, as a path unfolds. This is because it is not a path through a labyrinth, but through a multiplicity of labyrinths with an unstable relation to one another with regard to events: 'The labyrinths . . . in no way form an ordered series. They do not belong to a structure of carrying over; nothing of the one is rediscovered in the other, at least as long as each is formed as a sort of cyclone around a heart which is the encounter, whose effects he prolongs and which he flees' (36). This passage is a commentary on and a conclusion drawn from the 'acts' of a friend of Lyotard's as he passes a bad and good night pursuing, but never quite confronting a woman he was once in love with. The friend is gradually drawn into different structures: one free of the woman, then one reflecting on her in an abstract way, then one that seeks to remind him of her, and one that drives him to take a strange sort of revenge (that may also be an invitation).

Each change in structure or labyrinth is driven by an unpredictable encounter, such as happening on a picture that bears a likeness to the loved one, over which the friend has no control in terms of the pattern of behaviour that precedes it: 'It must not be said that the encounter takes place in the labyrinth; the labyrinth issues from the encounter' (36). Like the politics of libidinal economy, it is wrong to ask the question 'A labyrinth for whom?' at this point. There is no 'whom' independent of the encounters and the multiplicity of chaotically unfolding labyrinths. There is no person, people or laws of peoples independent of the encounters. The continuity of the friend as the person who experiences and acts, of Lyotard as observer, is illusory in terms of the moment of encounter of structures and intensities ('cyclone around a heart'). We – any people, or person – may derive a sense from Lyotard's account, but that sense is a false preparation for our own encounters and thereby it is also a false response to the encounters of others: 'There are only encounters, each tracing at full speed around itself a multitude of transparent walls, secret thresholds, open grounds, empty skies in which each encounter flees from itself, is forgotten, or is repeated – ceasing then to be an encounter' (36).

The principles of active passivity are important because they are directed away from the illusion of a valid permanence, whether a logical rule, a transcendent thing or a condition. These illusions reduce previous encounters to repetition, in the sense that the structures or labyrinths that they gave rise to are taken to be in some way impervious to new encounters of the radical form that Lyotard describes. This description is not allied to an argument for the value of radical encounters or events, as it is in Lyotard's later philosophy through the feeling of the sublime. It is allied to an observation of the nihilism that follows from the breaking of the illusion. A political identity in the form of a people or person negates discontinuity and impermanence, but thereby loses any defence against its return in the form of intensity: 'Always lost, even when we believe we make some sense of it, when, for example, we attribute such an emotion to an underlying support, to ourselves, to a person' (38). Not so much a libidinal politics for intensity and against structure, then, but a politics with intensity in structures, including those of person-hood and peoples if they happen to have a grip on us.

CONCLUSION

LYOTARD, TRUTH AND PRINCIPLES

What is the status of the concepts 'illusion' and 'false' in Lyotard's turn away from fixed identities and values? His work gives the consistent impression of an attack on mistaken and damaging beliefs, such as the belief in the subject or in a self that he tries to undermine through the principle 'seek anonymity by abandoning analysis'. This implies that he depends upon and can supply a sense of the true and the real as the contradiction of falsity and illusion. Yet standards of truth and reality are never given, if by them we understand definitions and arguments for their truth and existence. It could be argued that in the later work this is supplied by the sublime, but as I have shown, that traps him in the singular moment of the feeling of the sublime with no basis on which to extend it through time. There is a terrible solipsism to the work on the sublime that stops it from providing a basis of any kind for a politics.

Solipsism is not the main problem for the libidinal economic philosophy, in the sense that it never comes down to a feeling but rather to a set of concepts and principles that come out of an eclectic and indefinite series of discussions and observations. The eclecticism and lack of determinacy are signs of Lyotard's principles of active passivity at work in the philosophy that puts them forward; it has been swayed and directed by an openness to events and attacks on the forms that restrict it. The concepts and principles give the libidinal work an extension beyond singular occurrences, or cases, that the later work lacks. So, somewhat oddly, given the wild style of the earlier works and the more obviously philosophical roots of the later works, the libidinal philosophy stands up best from the point of view of a search for the most consistent and defensible philosophical and political position. Indeed, the main claim of this book, in terms of readings of Lyotard's work, is that his and other commentators' bias towards the later work is mistaken. In comparison to *The Differend*, *Libidinal Economy* is a more effective and careful response to the threat of the nihilism that can be traced back to Lyotard's early work on Algeria.

However, this sceptical and sometimes violent reaction to *Libidinal Economy* is easily understood, since it is invited by the book's attitude to argument and to the management of the feelings of its readers. It is provocative and can appear irresponsible, above all with respect to traditional ways of understanding truth and political action. I have considered the problems implied by this approach in terms of its arguments and status as theory in Chapter 3. The accusation that it is merely a fanciful metaphysics was answered in Chapter 4. The same chapter also responded to the problem of the apparent lack of positive direction for the philosophy and politics; this was tackled mainly in terms of the question of whether libidinal economics involves a collaboration with capitalism as opposed to a conspiracy within it. In Chapter 5, the problem of the lack of judgement and

143

the possible irresponsibility of the libidinal work was studied in the context of Lyotard's turn to judgement in his later work on the differend.

In each of these cases it became clear that answers to the problems were not lacking. Lyotard's work gave explicit grounds on which to develop positions that showed not only an awareness of the problems, but also a capacity to overcome them by developing a consistent philosophy and politics that I have characterised as active passivity. But, equally, it also became clear that these answers were unsatisfactory from the point of view of a philosophy and a politics that still clung to the possibility of, respectively: well-grounded and linear arguments that allowed absolutely certain conclusions to be drawn; a final distinction made between metaphysics and a pure positive philosophy that owed nothing to speculation and invention; an ideal political situation that gave direction to political struggles without owing anything to the states that it sought to resist or escape; just judgement, defined as a conscious and impartial capacity to decide upon the just and the true.

So the treatment of truth described at the outset of this section is paradigmatic of Lyotard's philosophy as a whole in that it is resistant to the demand for independent foundations for philosophical argument and political action. This is not the place to discuss that resistance in general; it is a trait and perhaps a weakness of many of the important strands of twentieth-century thought. However, his libidinal philosophy is of particular interest in two important ways. First, due to the direct way in which he presents his anti-foundational position, that is, through an engagement with political issues and common experiences without a search for a high poetic, or historical, or detached academic style of thought, Lyotard makes that position uncomfortable in a very brutal manner. There is no veil -- a novel and difficult style of thought -- hiding the implications of his libidinal philosophy. For each of the possibilities discarded above there is a raw and usually explicit result. Interpretation and argument become malign, requiring an antagonistic approach -- one that does not so much seek to follow and simply understand, as cynically make a place for new intensities and structures. Reality is made to coincide with metaphysical models in a way that elevates art above science, even in the realm of science (in economics, for example). Politics abandons conscious hopes and ideals, though not the structures in which those hopes and ideals are articulated. With that abandonment, there is also an openness to cruelty, defined precisely as an openness to intensities and their repercussions as painful change in a void of judgement.

Again, it is not the point here to seek to dismiss these results or judge them from a point of view that cannot accept how they are arrived at. Instead, I want to insist on the positive way they can be embraced as part of active passivity; that is, at least from the point of view of its principles and the affirmation of a radical openness, the results are necessary and to be welcomed since they contribute to our capacity to conduct new intensities, new feelings and desires into the political structures we live with. This is the second particular interest of Lyotard's anti-foundational philosophy: it goes further than merely accepting what we may commonly see as faults; it welcomes them and thereby escapes the nihilistic hubris of believing that we can live without them.

BIBLIOGRAPHY

Barthes, Roland 1980: *Sollers Écrivain*, Paris: Seuil.

Baudrillard, Jean 1972: *For a Critique of the Political Economy of the Sign*, trans. C. Levin. St Louis: Telos.

———— 1975: *The Mirror of Production*, trans. M. Poster. St Louis: Telos.

———— 1989: *America*, trans. C. Turner. New York: Verso.

Benjamin, Andrew (ed.) 1992: *Judging Lyotard*, London: Routledge.

Bennington, Geoffrey 1988: *Lyotard Writing the Event*. Manchester: Manchester University Press.

de Beistegui, Miguel 1998: *Heidegger and the Political*. London: Routledge.

Burroughs, William and Odier, Daniel 1970: *The Job: Interview with William Burroughs*. London: Cape.

Carroll, David 1987: *Paraesthetics: Foucault, Lyotard, Derrida*. London: Routledge.

Castoriadis, Cornelius 1973a: *L'Expérience du mouvement ouvrier*. Paris: Union Générale d'Éditions.

———— 1973b: *La société bureaucratique*. Paris: Union Générale d'Éditions.

Deleuze, Gilles 1983: *Nietzsche and Philosophy*, trans. H. Tomlinson. New York: Columbia University Press.

———— 1988: *Foucault*, trans. Seán Hand. Minneapolis: University of Minnesota Press.

———— 1990: *The Logic of Sense*, trans. M. Lester with C. Stivale. New York: Columbia University Press.

———— 1993: *Difference and Repetition*, trans. P. Patton. London: Athlone.

Deleuze, Gilles and Guattari, Félix 1977: *Anti-Oedipus: Capitalism and Schizophrenia*, trans. R. Hurley, M. Seem, H. Lane. New York: Viking.

———— 1987: *A Thousand Plateaus*, trans. B. Massumi. Minneapolis: University of Minnesota Press.

Deleuze, Gilles and Lyotard, Jean-François 1975: 'A propos du département de psychanalyse à Vincennes'. *Temps Modernes*, 342, 862–3.

Derrida, Jacques 1989: 'Some statements and truisms about neo-logisms, newisms, postisms, parasitisms, and other small seisms' in D. Carroll (ed.) *States of Theory*. New York: Columbia University Press.

Dews, Peter 1985: 'The "new philosophers" and the end of leftism' in R. Edgeley and R. Osborne (eds) *Radical Philosophy Reader*, pp. 361–84. London: Verso.

———— 1987: *Logics of Disintegration*. London: Verso.

Farias, Victor 1989: *Heidegger and Nazism*. Philadelphia: Temple University Press.

Ferry, Luc and Renault, Alain 1985: *La Pensée 68*. Paris: Gallimard.

Freud, Sigmund 1971: *Beyond the Pleasure Principle*, trans. J. Strachey. London: Hogarth Press.

Foucault, Michel 1978: *The History of Sexuality: an Introduction*, trans. R. Hurley. Harmondsworth: Penguin.

———— 1987: *The Use of Pleasure: the History of Sexuality, Volume 2*, trans. R. Hurley. Harmondsworth: Penguin.

———— 1988: *The care of the Self: the History of Sexuality, Volume 3*, trans. R. Hurley. New York: Vintage.

Grant, Iain Hamilton 1993: 'Introduction' in Lyotard 1993a.

Guyer, Paul 1997: *Kant and the Claims of Taste*. Cambridge: Cambridge University Press.

Heidegger, Martin 1977: *The Question Concerning Technology and Other Essays*, trans. W. Lovitt. New York: Harper and Row.

———— 1987: *Nietzsche: Volumes 1 to 4*, trans. D. F. Krell. New York: HarperCollins.

Kant, Immanuel 1978: *Critique of Pure Reason*, trans. N. K. Smith. London: Macmillan.

———— 1980: *Critique of Judgement*, trans. J. C. Meredith. Oxford: Clarendon Press.

———— 1990: *Political Writings*, ed. H. Reiss. Cambridge: Cambridge University Press.

Kemal, Salim 1997: *Kant's Aesthetic Theory*. London: Macmillan.

Lacoue-Labarthe, Philippe 1987: *La fiction du politique*. Paris: Christian Bourgois.

Lacoue-Labarthe, Philippe and Nancy, Jean-Luc (eds) 1981: *Les Fins de l'homme: à partir du travail de Jacques Derrida*. Paris: Galilée.

Lançon, Philippe 1996: 'Interview with J.-F. Lyotard', *Libération*, 23 November, 1996.

Lyotard, Jean-François 1948: 'Nés en 1925'. *Temps Modernes*, **32**, May, 2052–7.

———— 1954: *La Phénoménologie*. Paris: Presses Universitaires de France.

———— 1971: *Discours, figure*. Paris: Klincksiek.

———— 1973: *Dérive à partir de Marx et Freud*. Paris. Union Générale d'Éditions. 2nd edn with new preface Paris: Galilée 1994. (Trans. at 1984a.)

———— 1974: *Économie libidinale*. Paris: Minuit. (Trans. at 1993a.)

———— 1977a: *Instructions païennes*. Paris: Galilée.

———— 1977b *Rudiments païens*. Paris: 10/18.

———— 1977c: *Les Transformateurs Duchamp*. Paris: Galilée.

———— 1979a: *Au Juste*. Paris: Christian Bourgois. (Trans. at 1984b.)

———— 1979b: *La Condition postmoderne*. Paris: Minuit. (Trans. at 1985a.)

———— 1980a: *Des Dispositifs pulsionnels*, 2nd edn with a new preface. Paris: Christian Bourgois. (First edn, Paris: Union Générale d'Éditions 1973.)

———— 1980b: *La Partie de peinture*. Cannes: Maryse Candela.

———— 1983: *Le Différend*. Paris: Minuit. (Trans. at 1988a.)

———— 1984a: *L'assassinat de l'expérience par la peinture, Monory*. Talence: Le Castor Astral.

———— 1984b: *Driftworks*. New York: Semiotext(e).

Lyotard, Jean-François 1984c: *The Postmodern Condition: a Report on Knowledge*, trans. G. Bennington and B. Massumi. Manchester: Manchester University Press.

———— 1984d: *Tombeau de l'intellectuel et autres papiers*. Paris: Galilée.

———— 1985a: *Just Gaming*, trans. V. Godzich. Minneapolis: University of Minnesota Press.

———— 1985b: *Les Immatériaux*. Paris: Centre Georges Pompidou.

———— 1986: *L'Enthousiasme: la critique kantienne de l'histoire*. Paris: Galilée.

———— 1987: 'Sensus communis', in *Le Cahier du Collège International de Philosophie*, 3, 67–88. Paris: Osiris.

———— 1988a: *The Differend: Phrases in Dispute*, trans. G. Van Den Abeele. Manchester: Manchester University Press.

———— 1988b: *Heidegger et 'les juifs'*. Paris: Galilée.

———— 1988c: *L'Inhumain: causeries sur le temps*. Paris: Galilée. (Trans. at 1991.)

———— 1988d: 'L'Intérêt du sublime' in J.-L. Nancy (ed.) *Du Sublime*, pp. 149–77. Paris: Belin.

———— 1988e: *Peregrinations: Law, Form, Event*. New York: Columbia University Press. (This includes an excellent bibliography by Eddie Yeghiayan of works by and on Jean-François Lyotard. This resource is available in a constantly updated form on the Internet at http://sun3.lib.uci.edu/indiv/scctr/wellek/lyotard/index.html. This comprehensive site and its search engines are the standard for Lyotard bibliographies.)

———— 1989a: *La Guerre des Algériens: Écrits, 1956–1963*, ed. M. Ramdani. Paris: Galilée. (Trans. at 1993c.)

———— 1989b: *The Lyotard Reader*, ed. A. Benjamin. Oxford: Blackwell.

———— 1991a: *The Inhuman: Reflections on Time*, trans. Geoffrey Bennington and Rachel Bowlby. Cambridge: Polity Press.

———— 1991b: *Leçons sur l'analytique du sublime*. Paris: Galilée.

———— 1991c: *Lectures d'enfance*. Paris: Galilée.

———— 1993a: *Libidinal Economy*, trans. Iain Hamilton Grant. London: Athlone.

———— 1993b: *Moralités postmodernes*. Paris: Galilée. (Trans. at 1997.)

———— 1993c: *Political Writings*, trans. and ed. Bill Readings and Kevin Paul Geiman. London: UCL.

———— 1996: *Signé Malraux*. Paris: Grasset.

———— 1997: *Postmodern Fables*, trans. G. Van den Abbeele. Minneapolis: University of Minnesota Press.

———— 1998: *Chambre sourde: l'anti-aesthétique de Malraux*. Paris: Galilée.

Lyotard, Jean-François *et al.* 1988: *Les cahiers de philosophie, 5, Jean-François Lyotard: Réécrire la modernité*. Lille: Les cahiers de philosophie.

Makkreel, Rudolph 1990: *Imagination and Interpretation in Kant: the Hermeneutical import of the Critique of Judgement*. Chicago: University of Chicago Press.

Merleau-Ponty, Maurice 1966: *Sens et non-sens*. Paris: Nagel.

Nancy, Jean-Luc 1985: 'Dies Irae'. In Jacques Derrida (ed.), *La Faculté de juger*, Paris: Minuit.

———— 1991: 'Lapsus judicii', trans. D. Webb and J. Williams. *Pli: The Warwick Journal of Philosophy*, 3.2, 16–40.

Nietzsche, Friedrich 1961: *Thus Spoke Zarathustra*, trans. R. J. Hollingdale. Harmondsworth: Penguin.

———— 1968a: *The Will to Power*, trans. W. Kaufmann and R. J. Hollingdale. London: Weidenfeld and Nicolson.

———— 1968b: *Twilight of the Idols and the Anti-Christ*, trans. R. J. Hollingdale. Harmondsworth: Penguin.

Ramdani, Mohammed 1989: 'L'Algérie, un différend' in Lyotard 1989a, 9–31.

Readings, Bill 1991: *Introducing Lyotard: Art and Politics*. London: Routledge.

———— 1992: 'Pagans, perverts or primitives? Experimental justice in the empire of capital', in Benjamin 1991.

———— 1993: 'Foreword: the end of the political', in Lyotard 1993c.

Rorty, Richard 1989: *Contingency, Irony, Solidarity*. Cambridge: Cambridge University Press.

Sollers, Philippe 1970: *Nombres*. Paris: Seuil.

———— 1972: *Lois*. Paris: Seuil.

———— 1980: *H*. Paris: Seuil.

———— 1981: *Paradis I*. Paris: Gallimard.

———— 1990: *Drame*. Paris: Gallimard.

———— and Jean-Loup Houdebine 1980: 'La Trinité de Joyce'. *Tel Quel*, **83**, 36–88.

Williams, James 1998: *Lyotard: Towards a Postmodern Philosophy*. Cambridge: Polity Press.

INDEX

active passivity 57–61, 62–3; and art
64–5; and capitalism 76–89; and
collaboration 76–8; and conspiracy
140; and Freud 67–8; and painting
71–5; and political strategy 139; and
political structures 138–42; principles
of 58–61, 142; and nihilism 139; and
nostalgia 138; and the sublime 94–5;
and truth 88–9; and the withdrawal
from the political 138–40
Adorno, Theodor 64
affirmation 49, 53, 77, 87
Algeria 9–33, 38, 78–9, 90; and
capitalism 13–27; and the differend
9–13; and libidinal economy 23–32;
and truth 9–13
alienation 26–7
anamnesis 136–8
D'Ans, André-Marcel 122
anti-foundationalism 144–5
apathy 71–5, 88–9
Arendt, Hannah 106
Aristotle 101, 120
art 64–75, 78, 90, 104, 125, 129; and
anamnesis 137–8; and capitalism
78–9; and matter 132–4
Augustine 98–9
Au juste 97–101
Auschwitz 57, 113, 137
avant-garde 38, 45, 66

Barthes, Roland 65
Baudelaire 66
Baudrillard, Jean 31
de Beistegui, Miguel 55
Bennington, Geoffrey 17–19
biography 1
Bourdieu, Pierre 24

bourgeoisie 19–27; and revolution 21–2
Burroughs, William 64

Cage, John 48, 133
capitalism 13–27; 79–89; and Algeria
13–24; and energy 80–7; and the law
of equivalence 80–7; and limit
tendencies 85–7; and need 81–4
Cashinahua 98, 122
Castoriadis, Cornelius 31
Cézanne, Paul 66, 71–5, 133
Charcot 124
Chinese erotics 86–9
Cioran, E.M. 121
Colbert 84
colonialism 9–13, 21
commonplace 46
communication 7, 107
critique 28–33, 43–4, 52
cruelty 97, 100–1, 144

dance 45
Delaunay, Sonia 66
Deleuze, Gilles 44, 49, 53, 56, 62–3, 68,
74, 125
democracy 46; and the differend 120–2;
and narrative 121
depoliticisation 26–7
Derrida, Jacques 30, 42–4, 55, 137
desire 2, 3, 66–70, 81–9; and need 81–4
Dews, Peter 35–6
dialectics 43–4, 48
differend 4, 9; failure of a politics of
116–8; and judgement 108–10; and
libidinal economy 92–5; and nihilism
135; and revolution 32–2
dissimulation 44–9, 52, 59, 63, 76
Duchamp Marcel 133, 136

151

economics 13–14; and Algeria 13–27
event 45, 47, 90
explanation 3

feelings 2, 3; *see* desire; sublime
Ferry, Luc 34
Foucault, Michel 62–3
della Francesca, Piero 71
Freud, Sigmund 47, 51, 67, 84, 90, 129–30

game theory 87–8
Grant, Iain Hamilton 40–1
great zero 50–1, 56, 82–3
Guattari, Félix 44, 68, 74
Guiffrey, Georges 70–5
Guyer, Paul 107
Gysin, Brion 64

Habermas, Jürgen, 124
Hegel, G.W.F. 30, 103
Heidegger, Martin 54–59
heterogeneity 9
Houdebine, Jean-Louis 65
human rights 122–3

Ideas of reason 14, 114–16, 119; and humanity 119–20; and irony 122–4; and metanarratives 121
inhuman 120; and artificial intelligence 127; and humanity 125; and Idea of the human 126–7; and nihilism 131–2; and science fiction 127
invulnerability 140–1
irony 122–6

Joyce, James 65
judgement 89, 144; by analogy 110–12; and the differend 92–6; and libidinal economy 91–6; and political responsibility 97–101; without criteria 100–1

Kant, Immanuel 91, 94, 101, 119–20, 130, 134; and the bridge between faculties 103–5; and the gulf between faculties 102–3; and Ideas of reason 114–16; Lyotard's interpretation of 102, 107–10; and the need of reason 110–12; and *sensus communis* 105–7
Kemal, Salim 104–5, 107

Klein, Yves 70
Kubrik Stanley, 127

labyrinth 141–3
Leibniz, G.W. 39
Levinas, Emmanuel 101
Libidinal Economy 34–43; and style 39–43
libidinal economy 3; and Algeria 23–32; and capitalism 79–89; and the differend 92–5; and dissimulation 44–8; and judgement 91–5, 97–101; and lack of judgement 96–7; and nihilism 49–56; and truth 143–5
Liebeskind, Daniel 137
life 1–8
Lorenzetti, Ambrogio 71
Louis XIV 84

Makkreel, Rudolph 107
Malraux, André 1–8
Marx 15, 35, 41, 48, 90; and exchange-value and use-value 79–81
masses 23–4, 32–3
matter 132–4; and nihilism 133–4
melancholia 135–7
mercantilism 84–5
Merleau-Ponty, Maurice 72–5
metaphysics 34–5, 54–7
method 28–9, 41–4
Monory, Jacques 45, 66

Nancy, Jean-Luc 42
narrative 18, 121–2, 125
Newman, Barnett 91, 134
Nietzsche, Friedrich 10, 42, 46, 48, 49, 101
nihilism 5–8, 19, 41, 49–53, 62–3, 86, 125, 138; and capitalism 82–3; and Heidegger 54–6; and life 6; and matter 133–4; and power 63
nostalgia 136–9; and anamnesis 137–8; and nihilism 138
nouveaux philosophes 35–7

pagan 98; and paganism 99–100
painting 71–5, 78
parochialism 97, 99
passivity 3
peasantry 22–5
phenomenology 67; *see* Merleau-Ponty
phrase regimen 9

INDEX

Plato 101
political action 1
political community 101
political pragmatics 119–21; and
negativity 119–20
politics 2–8, 9, 135–45; and art 3, 4; and
the political 2–8; *see* active passivity;
differend
Pollock, Jackson 70
pop art 78
The Postmodern Condition 93
postmodernism 10, 15, 27; and the
inhuman 128–9
poststructuralism 1, 10, 35, 44–9
proletariat 20, 22–5
Proust, Marcel 48

quietism 97

racism 23
Ramdani, Mohammed 9–11, 36
Readings, Bill 17–19, 36–7
recollection 130
Renault, Alain 34
resistance 11, 78, 120, 130; and aesthetics
11
revolution 13–27, 78; and the
bourgeoisie 21–2; and the differend
32–3; in France 25–7
rewriting 129–30
Rorty, Richard 126

sado-masochism 86
Sartre, Jean-Paul 10
sensus communis 105–8, 111
sign 44–9, 50, 95; duplicitous, 52;
historical 114; and structuralism 44–9,
95
singularity 45

Socialisme ou barbarie 9, 11–12, 14, 23
solipsism 143
Sollers, Philippe 65
Spinoza, Baruch 48, 60
spontaneity 9, 10, 20, 22, 31
Stalinism 14
Stein, Gertrude 65
style 40–4; and *Libidinal Economy*
39–43; and irony 123–4
subject 1, 51–2, 59–60, 63, 71, 141–5
sublime 12, 23, 103, 113–14, 130; and
enthusiasm 115; and irony 124–6; and
matter 134; and nostalgia 137; and
performative contradictions 92–3

Taoism 86–9
technology 124–5
terror 15–19, 90
Thébaud, Jean-Loup 97, 101
theory 22, 41–4, 52, 59, 80, 141–5; and
anti-theory 63
totalitarian politics 121
Trotskyism 14
truth 1, 6, 7, 17, 143–5; and Algeria
9–13; and style 40–4
Turner, J.M.W. 4

untranslatability 18

Van Den Abeele, Georges 137
Varro 98
Versailles 85

Whiteread, Rachel, 137
will to power 50, 54–6
Wittgenstein, Ludwig 11, 91

Zeami 64, 66